Da

T0258326

'A beguiling play about a son's need
his father and himself . . . in a class w_____ ___ ____ __ ____
O'Casey' *New York Times*

Hugh Leonard's work includes the best-selling novel *A
Wild People* (2001) and two highly praised volumes of
autobiography, *Home Before Night* and *Out After Dark*. He
writes a weekly column in the *Sunday Independent*. He is an
award-winning playwright, screenwriter and novelist, and
was Literary Editor at the Abbey Theatre, Dublin from
1976 to 1977 and Programme Director of the Dublin
Theatre Festival. His many plays include the Tony Award-
winning *Da* (1973) and Tony-nominated *A Life* (1979), *A
Leap in the Dark* (1957), *A Walk on the Water* (1960), *The Saints
Go Cycling In* (1965), *The Au Pair Man* (1968), *The Patrick Pearse
Motel* (1971), *Thieves* (1973), *Summer* (1974), *Irishmen* (1975)
and *Time Was* (1976). Other works include the screenplay
for *Da* and the film *Widow's Peak* and television adaptations
include *Great Expectations*, *Nicholas Nickleby*, *The Moonstone*,
Wuthering Heights and *Good Behaviour*. His novelisation of his
four-part drama *Parnell and the Englishwoman* (BBC) won the
1992 Sagittarius Award. He lives in Dalkey, County Dublin.

by the same author and available from Methuen Drama

Memoirs
Home Before Night
Out After Dark

Fiction
A Wild People

Da

Hugh Leonard

Methuen Drama

Published by Methuen Drama

3 5 7 9 10 8 6 4

Methuen Drama
A&C Black Publishers Limited,
36 Soho Square,
London W1D 3QY

First published in 1973 by Penguin Books Ltd

A CIP catalogue record for this book is available from the British Library

ISBN 0 413 77277 2

Typeset by SX Composing DTP, Rayleigh, Essex
Printed and bound in Great Britain by
Cox & Wyman Ltd, Reading, Berkshire

The National Theatre
The Abbey and Peacock Theatres

Da

By Hugh Leonard

The National Theatre gratefully acknowledges the financial
support from the Arts Council/An Chomhairle Ealaíon

Da

By Hugh Leonard

This revival of **Da** by Hugh Leonard was first performed at the Abbey Theatre on Friday 5th July 2002. Press night was Wednesday 10th July 2002.

The Place – a kitchen and later, places remembered.

The Time – May 1968, and later, times remembered.

There will be one interval of 15 minutes

Cast

Charlie	Seán Campion
Oliver	Ronan Leahy
Da	Stephen Brennan
Mother	Anita Reeves
Young Charlie	Alan Leech
Drumm	John Kavanagh
Mary Tate	Jasmine Russell
Mrs Prynne	Deirdre Donnelly
Director	Patrick Mason
Designer	Paul McCauley
Lighting Designer	Paul Keogan
Sound	Cormac Carroll
Stage Director	Finola Eustace
Assistant Stage Manager	Catriona Behan
Voice Coach	Andrea Ainsworth
Set	Abbey Theatre Workshop
Costumes	Abbey Theatre Wardrobe Department
Casting Director	Marie Kelly

Please note that the text of the play which appears in this volume may be changed during the rehearsal process and appear in a slightly altered form in performance.

Stembridge (BBC), **Body in Hume Street** (RTE), **Fair City** (RTE), **Runway One** directed by David Drury (BBC) and more recently playing the vet, Siobhan, in **Ballykissangel** (BBC). Film work includes **Criminal Conversation** and **Attracta** directed by Kieran Hickey, **A Portrait of the Artist** directed by Joseph Strick, **The Fantasist** directed by Robin Hardy and **The Lilac Bus.**

John Kavanagh *Drumm*

John's previous performances at the Abbey and Peacock Theatres include **King of the Castle, "Moving", The Bird Sanctuary, The Well of the Saints** and **Wonderful Tennessee.** Other theatre work includes **The Plough and the Stars, Juno and the Paycock, One Flew over the Cuckoo's Nest,** Gaiety Theatre, **Juno and the Paycock,** Dublin/ New York, **The London Vertigo, A Month in the Country, Just Between Ourselves, Jane Eyre, The Weeping of Angels, A Streetcar Named Desire, Uncle Vanya, As You Like It, Taking Steps, The Norman Conquests, Twelfth Night, Absurd Person Singular,** Gate Theatre, and **The Homecoming** Gate, Dublin/New York/London. **Red Roses and Petrol** with Pigsback Theatre, **A Life,** Olympia Theatre. Musicals include **Les Miserables, Cabaret, Jacques Brel, HMS Pinafore, Pirates of Penzance, Tom Foolery, Innish, Hunky Dory** and **Guys and Dolls.** Television credits include **Sean, The Country Girls, Echoes, Ballroom of Romance, The Riordans** (RTE), **Fools of Fortune, Caught in a Free State, The Contractor, The Border Country, Investigation** and **Maigret** (Granada), **August Saturday, Children of the North, Arise and Go Now, Bad Company, Love Lies Bleeding, The Shadow of a Gunman, Vicious Circle** and **Rebel Heart** (BBC), **Dr Finlay's Casebook** (Scottish TV), **Scarlett, Sharpe's Gold** (Central TV). Films include **Joyriders, Cal, Into the West, Widow's Peak, Circle of Friends, Braveheart, Some Mother's Son, The Informant, The Butcher Boy, Sweeney Todd, This is My Father, Dancing at Lughnasa, Meteor, A Love Divided,** Puckoon, in **Sinners** (BBC) and **Benedict Arnold** (Braunstein Films).

Ronan Leahy *Oliver*
Ronan trained as an actor for three years and has been working professionally for over ten. Previous appearances at the Abbey and Peacock Theatres include **Living Quarters, Observatory, At Swim-Two-Birds, The Passion of Jerome, By The Bog of Cats, The Doctor's Dilemma, The Well of the Saints, Observe The Sons Of Ulster Marching Towards the Somme** and **Philadelphia, Here I Come!**. Other theatre includes **Carshow,** Corn Exchange, **Wideboy Gospel,** Bedrock Productions, **Melonfarmer,** Theatre Royal, Plymouth, **Easter Dues,** Bickerstaffe, **The Flesh Addict,** Pigsback, **Romeo and Julieta,** Theatro Potlacha, **Russian Tales** and most recently, **White Woman Street,** Meridian. Television and film credits include **On Home Ground,** RTE, **Studs,** Paul Mercier, **Coolockland,** RTE Short Cuts, **The Snare,** Cross Border Films and **Amongst Women,** BBC/RTE.

Alan Leech *Young Charlie*
Alan graduated in Drama and Theatre Studies, Trinity College Dublin. Previously at the Abbey and Peacock Theatres he performed in **The Morning after Optimism.** Other theatre work includes **A Streetcar Named Desire,** Gate Theatre, **This Lime Tree Bower** and **The Queen and the Peacock,** Red Kettle Theatre Company. Film credits include **Yesterday's Children, The Dentist's Daughter, The Escapist, Cowboys and Angels** and **Benedict Arnold.**

Anita Reeves *Mother*
Anita's appearances at the Abbey and Peacock Theatres include Kate in **Dancing at Lughnasa,** Mrs Malaprop in **The Rivals,** Meena in **Sive,** Maggie in **Dancing at Lughnasa** at the Abbey Theatre, Royal National Theatre and West End where she was nominated for an Olivier Award and received the Plays and Players Award for Best Supporting Actress, **You Can't Take it with You, Hatchet, A Flea in Her Ear** and **Moving.** Other theatre work includes The Inn Keeper's Wife in **Les Miserables,** Point Depot, Onoria in **Naked,** Almeida and West End, London, Kate in **The Cripple of Inishmaan,** Royal National Theatre, London and on tour in Ireland, Adelaide in **Guys and Dolls,** Gaiety Theatre, Ginnie Gogan in

The Plough and the Stars, UK tour and Garrick Theatre, London, Juno in **Juno and the Paycock,** Gaiety Theatre, UK tour and the West End, **Shirley Valentine,** Tivoli Theatre, **Absurd Person Singular, Taking Steps** and **The Norman Conquests,** all at the Gate Theatre, **A Life** and **The Pirates of Penzance** at the Olympia, **HMS Pinafore, A Day in the Death of Joe Egg** and two seasons of Panto at the Gaiety Theatre. Film and television includes **The American, The Butcher Boy, Talk of Angels, Scarlett, Into the West, The Miracle, Fools of Fortune, Angel** and **The Ballroom of Romance**. Anita lives in Dublin with her husband, Julian and their two children, Gemma and Danny.

Jasmine Russell *Mary Tate*
Jasmine began acting with the Dublin Youth Theatre. Work at the Abbey and Peacock Theatre includes **The Morning after Optimism, The Marriage of Figaro, Sheep's Milk on the Boil** and **The Comedy of Errors** at the Abbey. Other theatre work includes **Starchild,** Storytellers Theatre Company, **Wired to the Moon, Dream Frame,** Fishamble Theatre Company, **The Asylum Ball,** Calypso Theatre Company, **Getting the Picture,** Lyric Theatre, **Big Mom, Pilgrims, Lovechild,** 1992, Project Arts Centre, **Wave, Children of Eve,** Andrews Lane Theatre. Films include **Guiltrip, The Disappearance of Finbar, Widow's Peak** and **Moondance.** On television Jasmine appeared in **Family, Fair City, Making the Cut, Double Carpet, Black Day at Black Rock** and **No Tears.**

Amharclann Na Mainistreach
The National Theatre

SPONSORS

Aer Lingus
Anglo Irish Bank
Ferndale Films
Dr. A. J. F. O'Reilly
RTE
Smurfit Ireland Ltd
The Gulbenkian Foundation
The Irish Times

BENEFACTORS

Aer Rianta
AIB Group
An Post
Bank of Ireland
Behaviour and Attitudes
Electricity Supply Board
Independent News and Media, PLC
IIB Bank
Irish Life & Permanent plc
Pfizer International Bank Europe
Scottish Provident Ireland
SDS
SIPTU
Unilever Ireland Plc

PATRONS

J. G. Corry
Guinness Ireland Group
Irish Actors Equity
Gerard Kelly & Co
McCullough-Mulvin Architects
Mercer Ltd
Smurfit Corrugated Cases
Sumitomo Mitsui Finance (Dublin)
Total Print and Design
Francis Wintle

**SPONSORS OF THE NATIONAL
THEATRE ARCHIVE**

Jane & James O'Donoghue
Sarah & Michael O'Reilly
Rachel & Victor Treacy

FRIENDS OF THE ABBEY

Margaret Ball
Patricia Barnett
Mr. Ron Bolger
Mr. Hugh Boyle

Mrs. Patricia Browne
Mr. Bernard Brogan
Ms. Ann Byrne
Mr. Joseph Byrne
Ms. Zita Byrne
Ann & Eamonn Cantwell
Lilian & Robert Chambers
Ms. Orla Cleary
Claire Cronin
Monica Cusack
Mrs. Dolores Deacon
Paul & Janet Dempsey
Patricia Devlin
Karen Doull
Pauline Fitzpatrick
Paul & Florence Flynn
Ms. Christina Goldrick
Leslie Greer
Mrs. Rosaleen Hardiman
Sean & Mary Holahan
Brian Hewson
Elizabeth & Gerry Horkan
Mrs. Madeleine Humphreys
Ms. Eileen Jackson
Ms. Kate Kavanagh
Mr. Francis Keenan
Mr. Peter Keenan
Vivienne & Kieran Kelly
Joan & Michael Keogh
Donal & Máire Lowry
Mr. Fechin Maher
Una M. Moran
McCann FitzGerald Solicitors
Padraig McCartan
Ms. Ellie McCullough
Mr. Joseph McCullough
Berna McMenamin
Dr. Chris Morash
Mr. Frank Murray
Ann Nolan
Giuliano Nistri
Donal O'Buachalla
Paul O'Doherty
Mrs. Mary O'Driscoll
Ann O'Kennedy
Eugene O'Sullivan
Mr. Vincent O'Doherty
Mr. Andrew Parkes
Dr. Colette Pegum
Mr. Michael P. Quinn
Yvonne Redmond
Lillian Rohan
Mr. Noel Ryan
Breda & Brendan Shortall
Don & Maura Thornhill
Nuala Ward

Amharclann Na Mainistreach
The National Theatre

Da

Da was first produced outside the USA at the Olympia Theatre, Dublin, for the Dublin Theatre Festival, on 8 October 1973, with the following cast:

Charlie	Kevin McHugh
Oliver	Frank Kelly
Da	John McGiver
Mother	Phyl O'Doherty
Young Charlie	Chris O'Neill
Drumm	Edward Golden
Mary Tate	Dearbhla Molloy
Mrs Prynne	Pamela Mant

Characters

Charlie	**Young Charlie**
Oliver	**Drumm**
Da	**Mary Tate**
Mother	**Mrs Prynne**

Place
A kitchen and, later, places remembered.

Time
May 1968 and, later, times remembered.

Set
There are several playing areas. The main one is the kitchen. This is the kitchen–living room plus small hallway of a corporation house. An exit at the rear to the scullery. A hint of stairs running up from the hall. There are two areas at either side of the kitchen and a series of connecting steps and ramps which climb up and over, behind the kitchen. One of the two areas is the sea-front . . . it includes a park bench. Behind the sea-front, on the rising platforms, is the hilltop. On the other side of the stage is a neutral area, defined by lighting. This can be a number of locales as the script requires. (In the second act there is an ornamental bench there; the park bench is removed.) The kitchen, however, is the womb of the play.

Act One

Charlie, *overcoat on, is at the kitchen table, sorting letters, family papers, old photos, etc., into two piles. He finds one paper of interest and puts on his glasses to examine it. He then goes to the range and pours boiling water from the kettle into a teapot. He then picks up the teapot as* **Oliver** *comes to the door.*

He is **Charlie**'s *age – early 40s. His clothes are too neat for him to be prosperous; youthful bouncy step, handkerchief exploding from his breast pocket. He sees that the door is ajar. He knocks all the same.*

Charlie   Yes?

Oliver *is about to come in, but stops to remove a crêpe bow from the door.*

Yes, who is it?

Oliver *steps into the hall and coughs.*

(*Half to himself.*) I didn't ask how you are, but who you are. (*Then, seeing him.*) Oliver!

Oliver   Instant recognition. Oh-yes, full marks.

Charlie   You . . . good God.

Oliver (*careful speech, equal emphasis on each syllable*)   Well, I'm still a native-you-know. Not a globe-trotter like some. (*Almost wagging a finger.*) Oh, yes.

Charlie   Well, today's the day for it.

Oliver   Par-don me?

Charlie   Old faces. They've turned up like bills you thought you'd never have to pay. I'm on my own . . . come in. (*He puts the teapot down on the table.*)

Oliver   Won't intrude. Thought I'd offer my . . .

Charlie   Sure.

Oliver   For your trouble. (*Holding up the wreath.*) I took the liberty.

Charlie   That's damn nice of you, Oliver. Thank you.

Oliver   It was –

Charlie   He would have liked that.

Oliver   It's from the door.

Charlie   From . . . ? (*A loud laugh.*) I thought it was a . . . gift-wrapped Mass card. I mean, Masses in English, the priest facing you across the altar like a chef at a buffet luncheon . . . I thought it was one more innovation. (*Taking it purposefully.*) Yes, by all means. (*He drops it into the range.*)

Oliver   Gwendolyn – the wife-you-know – saw the notice in the 'Press'. I would have gone to the funeral –

Charlie   What for!

Oliver   But business-you-know.

Charlie   It's nice to see you. It must be ten . . . I don't know, fifteen years? Sit down . . . the mourners left a soldier or two still standing. (*He takes a bottle of stout out of a crate.*)

Oliver   It's seldom I take a drink.

Charlie   I've made tea for myself, do you mind? I never drink in this house. Every Christmas the Da would say: 'Will you have a bottle of stout, son?' Couldn't. It was the stricken look I knew would come on my mother's face, as if I'd appeared in my first pair of trousers or put my hand on a girl's tit in her presence.

Oliver (*dutifully*)   Ho-ho-ho.

Charlie   So I . . . (*Blankly.*) What?

Oliver   Joll-y good.

Charlie   My God, Oliver, you still think saying 'tit' is the height of depravity. You must find married life unbearably exciting.

Oliver (*beaming*)   Haven't changed, haven't changed!

Charlie (*pouring the stout*)   Anyway, I kept meaning to take that Christmas drink and send her upstairs in tears with a frenzied petition to St Ann. Next thing I knew, there I was aged thirty-nine, the year she died, a child on my lap who was capable of consuming the dregs of everyone else's tawny port to wild grandparental applause, and my wife sitting where you are, looking with disbelieving nausea at the man she had half-carried home the previous night, as he shook his greying head virtuously and said: 'No, thanks, Da, I still don't.' (*He hands the stout to* **Oliver.**) After she died, the not altogether frivolous thought occurred to me that the man who will deliberately not cause pain to his mother must be something of a sadist. I suppose I could have had a drink since then, but why spoil a perfect . . . (*Looking down at* **Oliver.**) You've got a bald spot.

Oliver   Me? No . . . ha-ha, it's the wind. (*Producing a comb.*) Breezy out. No, no: fine head of hair still-you-know.

Charlie *smiles and pours his tea, using a pot-holder.*

(*As he combs.*)   Warm for a coat, but.

Charlie   Yes.

Oliver   Month of May-you-know.

Charlie (*an evasion*)   I was halfway out the door when I remembered this lot. Rubbish mostly. HP agreements, rent books, insurance, broken pipe . . . (*He moves them to the bureau.*)

Oliver   Now!

Charlie   What?

Oliver (*bowing his head for inspection*)   Look, You see . . . See?

Charlie   Mm . . . you were right and I was wrong. Hair care is not an idle dream.

Oliver   The old massage-you-know.

Charlie   Ah-hah.

Oliver (*firmly*)   Oh, yes. (*Stroking his hair, he picks up his glass and drinks.*)

Charlie   Have you children?

Drinking, **Oliver** *holds up four fingers.*

Ah?

Oliver *jabs a finger towards* **Charlie**.

Charlie   Um? (*Takes a sip of tea.* **Charlie** *points interrogatively towards himself and raises one finger.*)

Oliver   Ah.

Charlie   What else?

Oliver   What?

Charlie   Is new.

Oliver   Oh, now.

Charlie   Long time. So?

Oliver   Oh, now. (*He thinks. Pause.* **Charlie** *waits, then is about to go back to his sorting.*)

Yes, by Jove, knew I had something to tell you. Six years ago . . .

Charlie   Yes?

Oliver   I finally got the theme music from 'King's Row'.

Charlie   Is that so?

Oliver   Only electronically-simulated stereo-you-know. But still . . .

Charlie   Still . . .

Oliver   That was a good fillum.

Charlie   Wasn't it.

Oliver   I got billy-ho for going with you to that fillum. My mother wouldn't let me play with you over that fillum.

Charlie   Why?

Oliver   Oh, pretend he doesn't know!

Charlie   Remind me.

Oliver   You made me miss my elocution class.

Charlie (*remembering*)   So I did.

Oliver   Ah, sappy days. Do you remember that expression we had, ah, sappy days? I was glad I kept up with the old elocution-you-know. A great stand-by. Always pronounce properly and look after your appearance: that's how you get on.

Charlie   *Did* you get on?

Oliver   Oh-well-you-know.

Charlie   How fantastic.

Oliver   No harm in being ready and waiting.

Charlie   None.

Oliver   That's why I was always smart in myself.

Charlie   And you got all the best girls.

Oliver   I did, though, did-n't I?

Charlie   Betty Brady . . .

Oliver   Oh, now.

Charlie   And that one who lived in the maze of buildings behind Cross Avenue. What was it we called her?

Oliver   The Casbah.

Charlie   The Casbah. And Maureen O'Reilly.

Oliver   Maureen . . . oh, don't-be-talking. There was a girl who took pride in her appearance. With the big – well, it was-you-know – chest.

Charlie   Tits.

Oliver (*as before*)   Ho-ho-ho.

Charlie   She once told me . . . she said: 'Oliver is going to be a great man.' Believed it.

Oliver*'s smile crumples; it is as if his face had collapsed from inside.*

Mad about you. They all were. What's up?

Oliver *shakes his head. He affects to peer closely at a wall picture.*

All I ever seemed to get was the kind of girl who had a special dispensation from Rome to wear the thickest part of her legs below the knees. (*Looking for reaction.*) Yes?

Oliver (*face unseen*)   Oh, now.

Charlie   Modelled yourself on Tyrone Power, right? I favoured Gary Cooper myself, but somehow I always came across as Akim Tamiroff. Jesus, Oliver, us in those days! We even thought Gene Autry could act.

Oliver (*turning*)   He could sing 'Mexicali Rose', still and all.

Charlie   Least he could do.

Oliver   Your drawback was you didn't take the Dale Carnegie course like I done.

Charlie   Too lazy.

Oliver   Very worthwhile-you-know. Then, after you went over the Pond, as they say, I joined the Rosicrucians. That was a great comfort to me the time the mother died. It's all about the soul surviving-you-know in the Universal Consciousness. Do you think I should keep on with it?

Charlie   Of course if it helps.

Oliver   Your da-you-know came to the mother's funeral. I never forgot that to him

Charlie   Well, he was always fond of you.

Da *comes in from the scullery and looks at* **Oliver**.

Da Fond of him? Fond of that one? Jesus, will you give over, my grave's too narrow to turn in. (*He goes out again.*)

Charlie, *in whose mind this has happened, winces.*

Charlie   In his way.

Oliver   In the end, was it . . . 'em, if you don't mind me asking . . . ?

Charlie   No, it wasn't sudden. He got these silent strokes, they're called. Old age. What I mean is, it wasn't unexpected. He *went* suddenly.

Oliver (*still delicately*)   You weren't, em . . .

Charlie   I was in London: flew over yesterday, off tonight. Well, my middle-aged friend, now we're both parentless. We've gone to the head of the queue.

Oliver   Queue for what? Oh, now. Long way to go yet, only getting started. (*He bounces to his feet.*) Well!

Charlie   Don't go. Finish your drink.

Oliver   The wife-you-know.

Charlie   Let me finish here and I'll run you home.

Oliver   No, must be riding the trail to the old hacienda.

Charlie (*a hint of urgency*)   Ten minutes.

Oliver   The little woman . . .

Oliver *moves to the door, takes gloves from his jacket pocket.*

Queer-you-know how a house looks empty after a funeral. What will happen to it now, do you think?

Charlie   This place? It'll be re-let, I suppose.

Oliver   I wondered – what was it I wondered? – do you happen to know anybody in the Corporation?

Charlie   Me?

Oliver   Well, I hear you got on, so they tell me.
Gwendolyn and me are on the list for a house this long time.
If you had a bit of pull-you-know.

Charlie (*his manner cooling*)   No, I haven't. Sorry.

Oliver   Oh, now. Man who's up in the world . . .

Charlie   I haven't.

Oliver   Oh. Well, ask not and you receive not.

Charlie   Dale Carnegie.

Oliver   Ho-ho. Oh, now. Well, see you next time you're
over. Sorry for the trouble. Sappy days, eh?

Charlie   Sappy days.

Oliver *goes.* **Charlie** *closes the door.*

Fucking vulture.

He faces the empty room. He returns the teapot to the range with
Oliver*'s unfinished tumbler of stout. He looks briefly at* **Da***'s chair*
and then goes to the bureau and begins to sort papers. He finds a wallet
and puts on his glasses to examine a photograph in it.

Da *comes in. He wears workingman's clothes: Sunday best.*

(*Refusing to look at him*)   Hoosh. Scat. Out.

Da   That wasn't too bad a day.

Charlie   Piss off.

Da *sits in his chair,* **Charlie** *looks at him.*

Sit there, then! No one is minding you.

Da   I knew it would hold up for you. You were lucky with
the weather when you came over at Christmas, too.

Charlie *ignores him and returns the papers to the table and goes on*
sorting them.

Mind, I wouldn't give much for tomorrow. When you can
see the Mountains of Mourne, that's a sure sign it'll rain.
Yis, the angels'll be having a pee.

Charlie (*whirling on him*)   Now that will do!

Da   That's a good expression. Did you ever hear that
expression?

Charlie   Did I? Thanks to you, until I was twelve years of
age every time the rain came down I had a mental picture
of a group of winged figures standing around a hole in the
clouds relieving themselves. Go away; I'm working, I'm
clearing up. (*Working, half to himself.*) Oh, yes, that was him. A
gardener all his life, intimately associated with rainfall: i.e.,
the atmospheric condensation of warm air which, when
large enough to fall perceptibly to the ground, constitutes
precipitation. Hot air rises, the rain falls; but as far as he was
concerned that kind of elementary phenomenon was . . .

Da   Codology.

Charlie   Codology. No, it was easier and funnier and
more theologically orientated to say that the angels were
having a pee.

He goes to the range and drops a large pile of papers in.

Da   You ought to put that down in one of your plays.

Charlie   I'd die first.

Da *rises and, without moving more than a step or two, takes a look at*
Charlie's *teacup, then turns towards the range.*

What are you doing?

Da   Sitting there without a cup of tea in your hand.

Charlie   I've a cupful.

Da   It's empty.

Charlie   It's full.

Da (*dismissively*)   G'way out that.

Charlie   Now don't touch that teapot. Do you hear me?
For forty-two years I've been through this, you and that
bloody teapot, and I know what's going to happen. So don't
touch it!

Da   Not a drop of tea in his cup . . . no wonder he's
delicate.

Charlie   Look, will you – (*He watches dumbly, almost tearfully,
as* **Da** *picks up the teapot and starts with it across the room. Halfway
across he sets the teapot down on the floor.*)

Da (*agonized*)   Jesus, Mary and Joseph. (*He hung his hand.*)

Charlie   I knew it.

Da, Charlie (*together*)   That's hot.

Charlie   Too damn headstrong. Couldn't you have
waited until my ma came in and let her – (*Softly.*) Jesus.

Da *begins to stalk the teapot.*

Da   Bad cess to it for an anti-Christ of a teapot. The
handle must be hollow. Whisht, now . . . say nothing. (*He
takes* **Charlie***'s cup from the table and looks contemptuously into it.*)
Empty! (*He pours the contents – it is three-quarters full – into a
scuttle, then kneels down, placing the cup in front of the teapot. He
holds the handle of the pot between fingers and thumb, using the end of
his necktie as a pot-holder, and pours the tea. Wincing.*) The devil's
cure to it, but it's hot. (*Rising.*) Oh, be the hokey. (*He sets the
cup before* **Charlie**.) There you are, son.

Charlie (*controlling himself*)   Thanks.

Da (*hovering*)   That'll put the red neck on you.

Charlie   Right!

Da   Where's the sugar?

Charlie   I have it. (*Beating him to the sugar and milk.*)

Da   Is there milk?

Charlie   Yes!

Da If you don't want tea I'll draw you a bottle of stout.

Charlie No! (*More composed.*) You know I never . . .
(*Correcting himself.*) I don't want a bottle of stout. Now sit.

Da Sure there's no shaggin' nourishment in tea. (*Returning to his chair, he is brought up short by the sight of the teapot.*) How the hell are we going to shift it? Hoh? If herself walks in on us and sees that on the floor there'll be desolation. The gee-gees let her down today, and if the picture in the Picture House was a washout as well she'll come home ready to eat us. That's a right conundrum, hoh?

Charlie (*coldly*) Cover it with a bucket.

Da The handle is hot for the night. (*A solution.*) Don't stir. Keep your ear cocked for the squeak of the gate.

Charlie Why? What . . .

Da *goes to the range, picks up a long rusting pair of tongs and starts to use them to lift the teapot.*

Oh, God. (**Charlie** *rushes over, grabs the teapot and puts it back on the range. He sucks his scorched hand.*)

Now will you get out and leave me be. You're dead. You're in Dean's Grange, in a box, six feet under . . . with her. I carried you . . . it's over, you're gone, so get out of my head.

Da *sits in the armchair, unperturbed, filling his pipe with tobacco.*

Or at least stay quiet. Eighty miserable years of you is in this drawer, and as soon as I've sorted out the odds and ends, I'm slamming that front door and that's *it*. Your nephew Paddy got the TV set, I gave the radio to Maureen and Tom, and Mrs Dunne next door got my sincere thanks for her many kindnesses and in consequence thereof has said she'll never talk to me again. The junkman can have the rest, because I've got what *I* want. An hour from now that fire will go out and there'll be no one here to light it. I'll be rid of you. I'm sweating here because I couldn't wait to put my coat on and be off. So what do you say to that?

Da (*amiably*)   Begod, son, you're getting as grey as a badger.

Charlie   Old Drumm was right about you. The day he came here to give me the reference.

Da   Drumm is not the worst of them.

Charlie   He had *you* taped.

Da   Was he here today?

Charlie   He was at the Mass . . . next to the pulpit.

Da   Was that him? I wouldn't recognize him. God, he's failed greatly.

Charlie   You can talk.

Da   Decent poor bugger, but.

Charlie   Do you know what he called you? The enemy.

Mother (*off*)   Charlie, will you come down when I tell you.

Charlie   Who's that?

Mother (*off*)   Charlie! (*She comes in from the scullery. At this time she is in her late 50s;* **Da** *is four years older.*)

(*Looking towards the ceiling.*) Do you want me to come up to you?

Charlie   I'd forgotten what she looked like.

Mother (*to* **Da**)   Will you get off your behind and call him. He's in the lavatory with his curse-o'-God books again.

Da (*galvanized into action, yelling*)   Do you hear your mother? Come down out of there. You pup, come when you're called. If I put my hand to you . . .

Mother   That will do.

Da (*now wound up*)   Slouching around . . . skipping and jumping and acting the go-boy. Mr Drumm is halfway up the path!

Mother   I said that will do. Read your paper.

Da (*a grotesque imitation of a boy leaping about*)   With your hopping and-and-and leppin' and your playing cowboys on the Green Bank. Buck Jones.

Charlie   You were always behind the times. I hadn't played cowboys in five years.

Da   Hoot-shaggin' Gibson, Tim McCoy and Randaloph Scott.

Mother   You'd give a body a headache.

Da (*subsiding*)   And-and-and-and Jeanie Autry.

Mother   When Mr Drumm comes in this house you're not to say yes, aye or no to him, do you hear me?

Da   Sure *I* know Drumm. Who was it pruned his rose-trees?

Mother   No passing remarks. (*She picks up the teapot.*)

Da   Mag, that teapot is . . .

Mother   Say nothing. (*She takes the teapot into the scullery.*)

Charlie   I never knew how she did it.

Da   'Tynan,' says he to me, ''clare to God, I never seen the beating of you for roses.' That's as true as you're standing there, Mag. Never seen the beating of me. (*Ruddy with pleasure.*) Hoh?

Charlie   Throw you a crumb and you'd call it a banquet.

Da   'I hear,' says he to me, 'you're a great man for the whist drives.' Do you know, I nearly fell out of my standing. 'Who told you that?' says I, looking at him. 'Sure,' says he, 'there's not a dog or divil in the town doesn't know you!' (*He laughs.*)

Young Charlie *comes downstairs. He is 17, shabbily dressed. He carries a book.*

(*To* **Young Charlie**)   Charlie, I was saying, sure I know old Drumm these donkey's years.

Charlie   Oh, God: not that little prick.

Young Charlie *looks at him, smarting at the insult. Their contempt is mutual.*

You were, you know.

Young Charlie   And what are you, only a big –

Charlie   Careful, that could lead to a compliment.

Young Charlie *sits at the table and opens his book.*

Da   Oh, Drumm will give you a grand reference.

Mother *returns with the teapot and pours boiling water into it.*

And if he didn't itself, what odds? Aren't we all grand and comfortable, owing nothing to no one, and haven't we got our health and strength and isn't that the main thing?

Charlie   Eat your heart out, Oscar Wilde.

Mother (*to* **Young Charlie**)   Don't lie over the table . . . You'll get a hump-back like old Totterdel.

Da   Old Totterdel was a decent man.

Charlie   What's the book?

Young Charlie (*surly*)   'Story of San Michele'. (*He pronounces it 'Michelle' as in French.*)

Charlie (*Italian*)   Michele, you thick.

Mother   The state of that shirt. I'll give you a fresh one.

Young Charlie   It's only Tuesday.

Mother   Take it off.

Young Charlie   How am I to wear one shirt all week?

Mother   You can go easy on it, can't you? Do as you're told. (*Going into the scullery.*) More you do for them, the less thanks you get.

Young Charlie *removes his shirt: under it is a singlet.*

Da   You could plant seed potatoes on that shirt, son.

Young Charlie (*muffled, the shirt over his head*)   Ah, dry up.

Da (*singing to himself: the tune is 'The Girl I Left Behind Me'*)
'Oh, says your oul' wan to my oul' wan,
"Will you come to the Waxie Dargle?"
And says my oul' wan to your oul' wan,
"Sure I haven't got a farthin'." '

The Waxies were tailors and the Waxie Dargle was a fair they used to have beyant in Bray in old God's time. You never knew that. Hoh?

Young Charlie, *shivering, ignores him.*

Charlie (*glaring*)   Answer him.

Young Charlie (*to* **Da**)   Yeah, you told me. (*To* **Charlie**.) You're a nice one to talk about being polite to him.

Charlie   Privilege of age, boy

Da (*pinching* **Young Charlie**'s *arm*)   Begod, son, there's not a pick on you. 'I'm thin,' the fella says, 'and you're thin'; but says he: 'Y'r man is thinner than the pair of us put together!'

Mother *has returned with the shirt.*

Mother   This is newly ironed. Put it on. (*She holds it for him. It has been lengthened by the addition of ill-matching pieces from another shirt to the tail and sleeves.*)

Young Charlie   What's that?

Mother   Put it on you.

Young Charlie   Look at it.

Mother   There's not a brack on that shirt, only it's gone a bit small for you. There's many a poor person 'ud be glad of it.

Young Charlie   Then give it to them.

Mother   You cur.

Young Charlie   God, look at the tail.

Mother   Who's going to see it?

Young Charlie   I'm not wearing it.

Mother (*flinging the shirt down*)   Leave it there, then. Don't. (*Picking it up at once.*) Put that shirt on you.

Young Charlie   I won't.

Mother (*turning to* **Da**)   Nick . . .

Da (*a half-feigned, half-real, rather frightened anger*)   Do like the woman tells you. Can we not have a bit of peace and quiet in the house the one day of the week? Jasus Christ tonight, do you want old Drumm to walk in on top of you?

Mother (*quietly*)   That will do with your Sacred Name. (*To* **Young Charlie**.) Lift your arms.

Young Charlie (*already beaten*)   I'm not wearing that –

She slaps his face briskly and, almost in the same movement, thrusts the shirt over his head. She pulls his arms into the sleeves, jerks him to her and fastens the buttons.

Da (*relieved*)   That's the boy. Herself cut up one of my old shirts for that, son: didn't you, Mag?

Charlie   You were always there with the good news.

Mother (*coldly, wanting to hurt back*)   The day you bring money in, you can start being particular. Time enough then for you to act the gentleman. You can do the big fellow in here then, as well as on the sea front. Oh, it's an old saying and a true one: the more you do for them . . .

Da   Sure that looks grand.

Mother   How bad he is . . . And at the end of it they'd hang you.

Young Charlie *puts his jacket on. He sits and picks up his book.*

Charlie   You always give in. Too soft to stand up to them. No guts.

Mother *is at the door looking out.*

It could have been worse. Like the time you had the date with Ita Byrne and you asked her (**Mother**.) to press your navy-blue trousers: told her it was for the altar boys' outing. She'd never pressed a pair of trousers in her life, and she put the creases down the side. And every little gurrier in the town followed you and Ita that night singing 'Anchors Aweigh'. Remember?

Young Charlie (*now grinning*)   Sappy days.

The gate squeaks.

Mother   There he is now. (*To* **Young Charlie**, *fearfully, the quarrel forgotten.*) God and his Holy Mother send he'll find you something.

Da *starts towards the door. She yanks him back.*

Will you wait till he knocks.

Da (*almost an incantation*)   Sure I know old Drumm.

Mother   And keep that mouth of yours shut. Have manners.

Young Charlie   He's only a clerk, you know.

She looks at him venomously. **Drumm** *comes into view: he is in his mid-50s, thin, acerbic. He knocks.* **Mother** *and* **Da** *go to the door. The greetings are mimed.*

Charlie   He was a chief clerk.

Young Charlie *looks towards the door, anguish on his face, fists clenched.*

Five-fifty a year . . . not bad for nineteen-forty . . . what?

Young Charlie   Four . . . November.

Charlie   What's up?

Young Charlie   Nothing.

Charlie   Don't be proud with me, boy.

Young Charlie   Listen to them: they always *crawl*.

Charlie   Blessed are the meek: they shall inherit the dirt. The shame of being ashamed of them was the worst part, wasn't it? What are you afraid of?

Young Charlie   Tell us . . . That day.

Charlie   When?

Young Charlie   Then. Now. Today. Did they . . . say anything to him?

Charlie   About what?

Drumm *is shown in.*

Mother   Still, we're terrible, dragging you out of your way.

Drumm   Is this the young man? (*Shaking hands.*) How do you do?

Da (*belatedly*)   Shake hands, son.

Drumm   A bookworm like myself, I see.

Mother (*to* **Da**)   Move out and let the man sit down.

Da (*offering his chair, saluting with one finger*)   Here you are, sir!

Charlie (*angry*)   Don't call him sir.

Mother   Now you'll sit there and have a cup of tea in your hand.

She sets about pouring the tea.

Drumm (*quite sternly*)   No, I will not.

Da (*aggressive*)   Don't mind him. Yes, he will. You will!

Drumm   You're a foolish woman. In these times we may take hospitality for granted. A ration of a half-ounce of tea per person per week doesn't go far.

Mother (*serving him*)   Now it won't poison you.

Da   And them's not your tea-leaves that are used and dried out and used again, sir. Get that down you. There's your milk and there's your sugar.

Drumm   Look here, my dear man, will you sit. I'm not helpless.

Mother   Nick . . .

Da   Sure what the hell else have we only for the cup of tea? Bugger all . . . amn't I right?

Drumm (*ignoring him, to* **Young Charlie**)   Your name is . . .?

Mother   Charles Patrick.

Drumm   And you've done with school?

Mother   He's got a scholarship to the Presentation Brothers. There was many a one got it and took the money; but no, we said, let him have the education, because it'll stand to him when we're gone.

Da   Oh, Charlie's the boy with the brains.

Drumm   Bright are you? Who's your favourite author?

Young Charlie   Shakespeare.

Charlie   You liar.

Drumm   And where do your talents lie?

Young Charlie   Dunno.

Drumm   An authority on Shakespeare shouldn't mumble. I asked, what kind of post do you want?

Mother   He'll take what he's offered. He's six months idle since he left school. He won't pick and choose.

Da   And if there's nothing for him, sure he can wait. There'll be any amount of jobs once the war's over.

Drumm   Past history says otherwise. There's usually a depression.

Da   Not at all.

Drumm   You're an expert, are you?

Da (*a stock phrase*)   What are you talking about, or do you know what you're talking about? The Germans know the Irish are their friends, and sign's on it, when the good jobs are handed out in England they'll give us the first preference.

Drumm   Who will?

Da   The Jerries, amn't I telling you . . . when they win.

Drumm   You support the Germans, do you?

Charlie (*to* **Da**)   Shut up. (*To* **Young Charlie**.) Don't go red. Smile.

Young Charlie *summons up an unnatural grin. He laughs. At once* **Drumm** *looks at him bad-temperedly.*

Drumm   Is something amusing you?

Young Charlie   No.

Da   Hitler's the man that's well able for them. He'll give them lackery, the same as *we* done. Sure isn't the greatest man under the sun, himself and De Valera?

Mother (*not looking at him*)   Now that will do . . .

Da   What the hell luck could the English have? Didn't they come into the town here and shoot decent people in their beds? But they won't see the day when they can crow it over Heil Hitler. He druv them back into the sea in 1940, and he'll do it again now. Sure what's Churchill anyway, bad scran to him, only a yahoo, with the cigar stuck in his fat gob and the face on him like a boiled shite.

Pause. **Drumm** *just looks at him.*

Mother   There's plenty more tea in the –

Drumm   No, I must be going.

Mother (*with a false smile*)   You oughtn't to mind him.

Drumm   I don't at all. I thought the boy might walk with me, and I could ask him what it is I need to know.

Mother   Charlie, do you hear? Go and comb your hair and give your face a rub.

Young Charlie *goes upstairs, glad to get away.*

I know you'll do your best for him. You will.

Drumm   It would be a poor best. There's nothing here for anyone. Have you thought of letting him go to England?

Da   England!

Drumm   There's work there.

Mother   Ah, no.

Drumm   It might be for his good.

Mother   No, we'd think bad of losing him.

Da   There's good jobs going here if you keep an eye out. I'm gardening above in Jacob's these forty-six years, since I was a young lad . . . would you credit that?

Drumm   Yes, I would.

Mother   What is there in England only bombs and getting into bad health? No, he'll stay where he's well looked after. Sure, Mr Drumm, we're all he has. His own didn't want him.

Drumm   His own?

Mother (*bitterly*)   Whoever she was.

Drumm   Do you mean the boy is adopted?

Young Charlie *comes downstairs at a run, anxious to be off. He hears what* **Drumm** *has said and hangs back on the stairs.*

Mother (*purely as punctuation*)   Ah, don't talk to me.

Charlie   And I listened, faint with shame, while you delivered your party-piece.

Mother   I took him out of Holles Street Hospital when he was ten days old, and he's never wanted for anything since. My mother that's dead and gone, the Lord have mercy on her, said to me: 'Mag, he's a nurse-child. You don't know where he was got or how he was got, and you'll rue the day. He'll turn on you.

Da (*a growl*)   Not at all, woman.

Mother   Amn't I saying! (*To* **Drumm**.) You try rearing a child on thirty shillings a week then and two pounds ten now after forty years of slaving, and see where it leaves you.

Charlie   Stand by. Finale coming up.

Mother   And a child that was delicate. She tried to get rid of him.

Drumm   Get rid?

Charlie   Roll of drums, *and* . . .!

Mother   Before he was born. Whatever kind of rotten poison she took. Dr Enright told me; he said, 'You won't rear that child, ma'am, he'll never make old bones.' But I did rear him, and he's a credit to us.

Charlie   Band-chord. Final curtain. Speech!

Mother   He's more to us than our own, so he is.

Charlie   Thunderous applause. (*To* **Drumm**.) Hand her up the bouquet.

Drumm   You're a woman out of the ordinary. The boy has cause to be grateful.

Charlie   Well done. House-lights.

Young Charlie, *his lips pressed tight together to suppress a howl, emits a high-pitched half-whimper, half-squeal, and flees into the garden.*

And the scream seemed to come through my eyes.

Mother   Charlie?

Drumm (*looking out*)   I see he's leading the way. Goodbye, Mrs Tynan: I'll do what little I can.

Mother   Sure I know. God never let me down yet.

Da (*he looks at* **Da** *and then at* **Mother**)   You surprise me.

Mother   Nick, say goodbye.

Da   Are you off? Good luck, now. (*Giving him a Nazi salute.*) We shall rise again. Begod, we will.

Drumm   You're an ignorant man. (*He nods to* **Mother** *and goes out.*)

Da *laughs softly and shakes his head, as if he had been complimented.*

(*Off.*)   Young man, come here.

Da (*as* **Mother** *comes in from hall*)   There's worse going than old Drumm. A decent man. 'I never seen the beating of you,' says he, 'for roses.'

She glares at him, too angry to speak, and takes **Drumm**'s *teacup out to the scullery.*

Charlie (*to* **Da**)   You could have stopped her. You could have tried. You never said a word.

Da (*calling to* **Mother**)   I think I'll do me feet tonight, Mag. I have a welt on me that's a bugger.

Charlie   All those years you sat and looked into the fire, what went through your head? What did you think of? What thoughts? I never knew you to have a hope or a dream or say a half-wise thing.

Da (*rubbing his foot*)   Aye, rain tomorrow.

Charlie   Whist drive on Wednesday, the Picture House on Sundays and the Wicklow regatta every first Monday in August. Bendigo plug-tobacco and 'Up Dev' and 'God bless all here when I get in meself'. You worked for fifty-eight years, nine hours a day, in a garden so steep a horse couldn't climb it, and when they got rid of you with a pension of ten shillings a week you did hand-springs for joy because it came from the Quality. You spent your life sitting on brambles, and wouldn't move in case someone took your seat.

Da (*softly*)   You're a comical boy.

Charlie (*almost an appeal*)   You could have stopped her.

Mother *comes in.*

Mother   Ignorant, he said you were, and that's the word for you.

Da (*taken aback*)   What?

Mother   With your 'Up Hitler' in front of him and your dirty expressions. Ignorant.

Da   What are you giving out about?

Mother   You. You sticking your prate in where it's not wanted, so's a body wouldn't know where to look. I said to you: 'Keep that mouth of yours shut,' I said. But no . . . it'd kill you.

Da   Sure I never said a word to the man, good, bad or indifferent.

Mother   You're not fit to be let loose with respectable people. I don't wonder at Charlie running out of the house.

Da   What? Who did?

Mother   It wouldn't be the first time you made a show of him and it won't be the last. God help the boy if he has you to depend on.

Da (*upset*)   Ah now, Mag, go easy. No . . . sure Charlie and me is –

Mother   *Anyone* would be ashamed of you.

Da   No, him and me is –

Mother   He's done with you now. Done with you. (*She goes out.*)

Charlie   Serves you right. You could have stopped her.

The lights go down on the kitchen and come up on the promenade. The sound of seagulls. **Drumm** *and* **Young Charlie** *appear. They stand in front of a bench.*

Drumm   The wind has moved to the east. Do you take a drink?

Young Charlie   Not yet.

Drumm   You will, please God. Do you chase girls?

Young Charlie   Pardon?

Drumm   Female persons. Do you indulge?

Young Charlie   The odd time.

Drumm   As a diversion I don't condemn it. Henry Vaughan, an otherwise unremarkable poet of the seventeenth century, summed it up happily when he wrote 'How brave a prospect is a bright backside.' Do you know Vaughan?

Young Charlie   'They are all gone into the world of light.'

Drumm   So you do read poetry! Listen to me, my friend: if you and I are to have dealings you had better know that I do not tolerate liars. Don't try it on with me ever again.

Young Charlie   I didn't . . .

Drumm (*firmly*)   Shakespeare is nobody's favourite author. (*He gives* **Young Charlie** *a searching look.*) We'll say no more about it. Yes, chase away by all means and give them a damn good squeeze if you can catch them, but be slow to marry. The maximum of loneliness and the minimum of privacy. I have two daughters myself . . . no boys.

Young Charlie   I know your daughters.

Drumm   Oh?

Young Charlie   To see. Not to talk to.

Drumm   I would describe them as . . . bird-like.

Young Charlie (*trying to say the right thing*)   Yes, I suppose they –

Drumm   Rhode Island Reds. You may laugh . . .

Young Charlie   I wouldn't.

Drumm   I say you may. *I* do. No . . . no boys. (*He sits on the bench and motions for* **Young Charlie** *to sit beside him.*) There will be a vacancy in my office for a filing clerk. I don't recommend it to you: jobs are like lobster pots, harder to get out of than into, and you seem to me to be not cut out for clerking. But if you want to sell your soul for forty-five shillings a week I daresay my conscience won't keep me awake at nights.

Young Charlie   Do you mean I can have it?

Drumm   If you're fool enough. My advice –

Young Charlie   A job. A job in an office, in out of the cold. Oh, Jancy, I think I'll go mad. (*He jumps up.*) Yeow!

Drumm *taps the umbrella on the ground.*

God, I think I'll split in two. I'm a millionaire Mr Drumm
. . . any time if there's e'er an oul' favour I can do for you
over this –

Drumm   You can speak correct English.

Young Charlie   Honest to God, Mr Drumm, I'm so
delighted, if you asked me to I'd speak Swahili. A job!

Drumm (*sourly*)   And this is how we throw our lives away.

Young Charlie (*grins, then*)   Beg your pardon?

Drumm   You'll amount to nothing until you learn to say
no. No to jobs, no to girls, no to money. Otherwise, by the
time you've learned to say no to life you'll find you've
swallowed half of it.

Young Charlie   I've been looking for a job since school,
Mr Drumm. I couldn't refuse it.

Drumm   To be sure.

Young Charlie   I mean, I'm the only one at home . . .

Drumm   I'm aware of that. (*Considers it settled.*) So be it.
There's a grey look about your face: I suggest you begin to
wash yourself properly. And I'll need a copy of your birth
certificate. What's your name?

Young Charlie (*surprised*)   Tynan.

Drumm   I mean your real name. You overheard what
your foster-mother told me, didn't you? That you're
illegitimate. Don't give me that woe-begone look. It's a fact,
you're going to have to live with it and you may as well
make a start. Bastardy is more ignominious in a small town
than in a large one, but please God it may light a fire under
you. Do your friends know?

Young Charlie *shakes his head.*

Probably they do. So don't tell them: they won't thank you
for spiking their guns. What ails you? Look here, my friend:
tears will get no sympathy from me. I said we'll have done

with it . . . people will take me for a pederast. Your nose is
running: wipe it.

Young Charlie   I haven't got a handkerchief.

Drumm   Well, you can't have mine. Use something . . .
the tail of your shirt.

Young Charlie *is about to comply when he remembers.*

Well?

Young Charlie   I won't.

Drumm (*bristling*)   Won't?

Young Charlie (*loftily*)   It's a disgusting thing to do.

Drumm   You think so?

They outglare each other. **Young Charlie** *sniffs deeply. Brass band
music is heard in the distance.*

Well, perhaps there's hope for you yet.

Young Charlie   There's a band on the pier.

Drumm (*rising to look*)   Hm? Yes, the boys from the
orphanage, by the sound of them.

Young Charlie *whips out his shirt-tail, wipes his nose and
readjusts his dress as* **Drum** *turns to face him.*

Your . . . mother, shall we call her? . . . is a fine woman.

Young Charlie   Yeah. Except she tells everyone.

Drumm   About you?

Young Charlie   All the old ones. Then they say to her:
isn't she great and how I ought to go down on my bended
knees. Even the odd time I do something right, it's not
enough . . . it's always the least I could do. Me da is
different: if you ran into him with a motor car he'd thank
you for the lift.

Drumm   I'm fond of him.

Young Charlie (*disbelieving*)   Of me da?

Drumm   I can afford that luxury: I'm not obliged to live with him. You are. That's why he's the enemy.

Young Charlie   The what?

Drumm   Your enemy.

Young Charlie (*straight-faced, trying not to laugh*)   I see.

Drumm   Don't be polite with me, my friend, or you'll be out of that job before you're into it. Once at a whist drive I heard him say that the world would end in 1940. It was a superstition that had a fashionable currency at one time among the credulous. Well, 1940 came and went, as you may have noticed, and finding myself and the county of Dublin unscathed, I tackled him on the subject. He was unruffled. He informed me that the world hadn't ended because the German bombs had upset the weather.

Young Charlie *laughs boisterously. He bangs his fists on his knees.* **Da** *enters the neutral area and rings a doorbell.*

Yes, the dangerous ones are those who amuse us.

The bell is rung again. **Da** *puts his pipe in his pocket and waits.*

There are millions like him: inoffensive, stupid, and not a damn bit of good. They've never said no in their lives or to their lives, and they'd cheerfully see the rest of us buried. If you have any sense, you'll learn to be frightened of him.

A light is flashed on **Da**'*s face as if a door had been opened.*

Da (*saluting*)   That's a hash oul' day, ma'am. Certainly you know me . . . Tynan, of Begnet's Villas, sure I'm as well known as a begging ass. And do you know what I'm going to tell you? . . . that back field of yours, the meadow: if you was to clear that field of the rocks that's in it and the stumps of trees and had it dug up with a good spreading of manure on the top of it, begod, you wouldn't know yourself. There's bugger-all you couldn't grow in it.

Drumm   From people too ignorant to feel pain, may the good God deliver us!

Da   The young lad, do you see, he's starting work. Oh, a toppin' job: running an office, sure he's made for life. And the way it is, I'd think bad of him starting off without a decent suit on his back or the couple of good shirts. Sure you couldn't let him mix with high-up people and the arse out of his trousers. Have you me?

Drumm   I'm advising you to live in your own world, not with one foot in his.

Da   I'll come to you so on Sundays and do the field . . . sure it won't take a feather out of me. (*Embarrassed by mention of money.*) Very good, yis . . . I'll leave that to yourself: sure whatever you think. (*Saluting.*) Thanks very much, more power. (*He starts off, then bobs back again.*) More power, says oul' Power when young Power was born, wha'?

The door-light snaps on. As he moves away, the lights on the neutral area go down.

Drumm   Are we still on speaking terms?

Young Charlie (*hating him*)   Yes.

Drumm   You aren't angry?

Young Charlie   No!

Drumm   Indeed, why should you be! Shall we stroll down and listen to the orphans?

*They walk off. Lights come up quickly on **Charlie** and **Da** in the kitchen as before.*

Charlie   And I went off with him like a trollop.

Da   Drumm is a decent skin. Came in here once to see how I was managing after herself died. Three years ago this month, yis. Gev me a packet of cigarettes. 'No,' says I, 'I won't.' 'You will,' says he; 'take them when you're told to.' So I did. Wait now till I see where I have them.

Charlie   We listened to the band and I even made excuses for you. Told him about your grandfather and two uncles starving to death in the Famine.

Da   Oh, aye. Them was hard times. They died in the ditches.

Charlie   What ditches? I made it up!

Da   Fierce times they were. Where the hell did I put them? You can smoke them in the aeroplane. (*Going to the dresser.*)

Charlie   I don't want them.

Da (*searching*)   Yes, you do.

Charlie   Don't make a – (*He takes a packet of 'Players' from his pocket.*) It's all right . . . look, I found them.

Da   Hoh?

Charlie   Look.

Da   Good lad. Yis, it was in the month of – (*He breaks off.*) Drumm smoked 'Sweet Aftons' . . . that's not them. (*He resumes the search.*)

Charlie   Messer!

Da   It was in the month of May herself died, and it was in the month of May I went. Would you credit that? (*He climbs on a chair.*)

Charlie   Congratulations. I should have stuck up for you and told him to keep his job. Then I could have hated you instead of myself. Because he was dead on: he described you to a – (*Seeing him.*) Oh, get down.

Da finds the cigarettes on top of the dresser. He begins to climb down.

You destroyed me, you know that? Long after I'd quit the job and seen the last of Drumm, I was dining out in London: black dickie-bow, oak panelling, picture of Sarah Bernhardt at nine o'clock: the sort of place where you have to remember not to say thanks to the waiters. I had just propelled an erudite remark across the table and was about to shoot my cuffs, lose my head and chance another one, when I felt a sudden tug as if I was on a dog-lead. I looked, and there were you at the other end of it. Paring your corns, informing me that bejasus the weather would hold up if it didn't rain, and sprinkling sugar on my bread when Ma's back was turned.

Da *gives him the cigarettes as if he was passing on contraband.*

Da   Say nothing. Put this in your pocket.

Charlie   So how could I belong there if I belonged here?

Da   'Take them,' says Drumm to me, 'when you're told to.'

Charlie   And it was more than a memory. She was dead then, and at that moment I knew you were sitting here on your own while the daylight went. Did you think bad of me? I wish I were a fly inside your head, like you're a wasp inside of mine. Why wouldn't you come and live with us in London when we asked you?

Da   What would I do that for?

Charlie   You were eighty-one.

Da   Sure I was a marvel. 'Begod, Tynan,' says Father Kearney to me, 'we'll have to shoot you in the wind-up.' What a fool I'd be to leave herself's bits and pieces here where any dog or divil could steal them. And for what? To go to England and maybe land meself in an early grave with the food they serve up to you.

Charlie   No, you'd rather stay here instead, like a maggot in a cabbage, and die of neglect.

Da   I fended for meself. No better man.

Charlie   In sight or out of it, you were a millstone. You couldn't even let me lose my virginity in peace.

Da   Lose your what?

Charlie   Nothing. It's a slang word, now obsolete.

Mary Tate *walks on. She is 25, a loner.*

Da   Who's that? That's a fine figure of a girl. What's she doing around here?

Charlie   She's not here: she's on the sea-front. And she wasn't a fine girl. She was known locally as the Yellow Peril.

Young Charlie *and* **Oliver** *– younger now – are lounging in the neutral area.* **Mary** *walks by. They pay her no obvious attention.*

Young Charlie *(suddenly, singing)*   'Underneath the lamplight . . .'

Oliver   'By the barracks gate . . .'

Young Charlie   'Darling, I remember . . .'

Oliver   'The way you used to wait.'

Young Charlie, Oliver *(together)*

'I heard you walking in the street,
I smelt your feet,
But could not meet,
My lily of the lamplight,
My own Lily Marlene.'

Mary's *step falters as she hears the lyric. She continues on to the bench, where she sits and opens a copy of 'Modern Screen'.*

The two youths go on singing – quietly now and to themselves.
Young Charlie *looks covertly at her once or twice.*

Charlie *(to* **Da**)   We all dreamed, privately and sweatily, about committing dark deeds with the Yellow Peril. Dark was the word, for if you were seen with her, nice girls would shun you and tell their mothers, and their mothers would tell yours: the Yellow Peril was the enemy of mothers. And the fellows would jeer at you for your beggarman's lust – you with your fine words of settling for nothing less than Veronica Lake. We always kept our sexual sights impossibly high: it preserved us from the stigma of attempt and failure on the one hand, and success and mortal sin on the other. The Yellow Peril never winked, smiled or flirted: the sure sign of an activist. We avoided her, and yet she was a comfort to us. It was like having a trusty flintlock handy in case of necessity.

Young Charlie *and* **Oliver** *both look at* **Mary**.

Young Charlie   They say she's mustard.

Oliver   Oh, yes. Red-hot-you-know.

Young Charlie   And she has a fine-looking pair.

Oliver   Of legs-you-mean?

Young Charlie   Well, yeah: them, too.

Oliver   Oh. Ho-ho-ho. Oh, now. Joll-y good.

Mary *looks up from her book as* **Oliver** *raises his voice: a calm direct look, neither friendly nor hostile.*

Young Charlie   She's looking. (*To* **Mary**, *bravely.*) 'Evening.

Oliver (*embarrassed*)   Don't.

Young Charlie   Why?

Oliver   We'll get ourselves a bad name. Where was I? Yes . . . I was telling you about Maria Montez in 'Cobra Woman'. Now there's a fine figure of a –

Young Charlie   They say she'd let you. All you have to do is ask.

Oliver   Maria Montez? Is that a fact?

Young Charlie (*pointing*)   Her.

Oliver   Ah, yes: but who is that hard up for it?

Charlie   I was.

Oliver   I mean, who wants to demean himself?

Charlie   I did.

Young Charlie   God, I wouldn't touch her in a fit. I'm only –

Oliver   And she would make a holy show of you, you-know, like she done with the man who tried to interfere with her in the Picture House.

Young Charlie   When?

Oliver   I think it was a Bette Davis. The man sat down next to her and as soon as the big picture came on the screen he started tampering with her in some way. And she never said a word, only got up and dragged him to the manager by his wigger-wagger.

Young Charlie (*stunned*)   She never.

Oliver   True as God. He felt very small, I can tell you.

Young Charlie   Still, if she minded she can't be all that fast.

Oliver   Oh-I-don't-know. If she wasn't fast she'd have dragged him by something else.

Young Charlie *looks at* **Mary** *in awe.*

Charlie   Lust tied granny-knots in my insides. I wanted the Yellow Peril like I wanted no girl before or no woman since. What was worse, I was wearing my new suit for the first time and I had to do it now, now or never, before the newness wore off.

Oliver (*who has been talking*)   So will we trot up to the billiard hall?

Young Charlie   You go.

Oliver   Me?

Young Charlie   I'll follow you. (*He looks almost tragically at* **Oliver**.)

Pause. Then **Oliver** *stares from him to* **Mary**.

Oliver   Her?

Young Charlie (*agonized*)   Go on.

Oliver   Ho-ho-ho-ho. Oh, now. (*Dismay.*) You wouldn't.

Young Charlie   Olly . . . fizz off.

Oliver   But you don't want to chance your arm with her; she'd *let* you. (*Then.*) Where will you take her?

Young Charlie   I dunno: down the back.

Oliver   I'll see you, then.

Young Charlie   Yeah.

Oliver   I suppose you know you'll destroy your good suit.

Young Charlie   Will you go on. See you.

Oliver *does not move. Hostility forms on his face.*

Oliver   I was the one you came out with-you-know.

Young Charlie *waits for him to go.*

They say it's very disappointing-you-know, very over-rated. (*Pause. Angrily.*) Well, don't salute me in the town when you see me, because you won't be saluted back. (*He goes.*)

Young Charlie *goes towards the bench. He stops, suddenly panic-stricken.*

Charlie *has by now moved out of the kitchen area.*

Charlie   Do you want a hand?

Still looking at **Mary**, **Young Charlie** *motions to him to be quiet.*

If they think you're afraid to ask them they attack you. You said yourself, all you have to do is ask.

Young Charlie   Dry up, will you.

Mary *looks at him.*

Charlie   Now . . . quick!

Young Charlie   'Evening.

Mary   You said that.

Charlie   Sit.

Young Charlie *sits beside her. What follows is ritual, laconic and fast.*

Mary   Didn't ask you to sit down.

Young Charlie   Free country.

Mary   Nothing doing for you here.

Young Charlie   Never said there was.

Mary   Ought to have gone off with that friend of yours.

Young Charlie   Who ought?

Mary   You ought.

Young Charlie   What for?

Mary   Nothing doing for you here.

Young Charlie   Never said there was.

Pause. Phase Two in conversation.

Mary   What's your name, anyway?

Young Charlie   Bruce.

Mary (*a sceptical grin*)   Yeah?

Young Charlie   It is. (*He crosses his eyes and thumbs his nose at* **Charlie** *by way of defiance.*)

Mary   Bruce?

Young Charlie   Mm.

Mary   Nice name.

Young Charlie (*pointing off*)   He's Oliver.

Mary   That so?

Young Charlie   He's from the town.

Mary   Where *you* from?

Young Charlie   Trinity College.

Mary   That right?

Young Charlie   English Literature.

Mary   Must be hard.

Young Charlie   Bits of it.

She goes back to her reading. A lull. End of Phase Two.

Charlie   Ask her.

Young Charlie   She's not on.

Charlie   Ask.

Instead, **Young Charlie** *clamps his arm heavily around* **Mary**. *She does not look up from her magazine during the following.*

Mary   Wouldn't Edward G. Robinson put you in mind of a monkey?

Young Charlie   Let's see. Do you know, he does.

Mary   One of them baboons.

Young Charlie   Yes. Yes, yes, yes, yes. (*At each 'yes' he slaps her vigorously on the knee.*)

She stares as if mesmerized at his hand as it bounces up and down and finally comes to rest on her knee in an iron grip. As she returns to her magazine he begins to massage her kneecap.

Charlie (*staring*)   You insidious devil, you.

Mary   It doesn't screw off.

Young Charlie   What?

Mary   Me leg.

His other hand now slides under her armpit, intent on touching her breast. He is unaware that he is kneading and pinching her handbag, which is tucked under her arm. She watches this hand, fascinated.

Charlie   I think you're getting her money excited.

Mary (*having returned to her reading*)   You needn't think there's anything doing for you here.

Young Charlie   I don't.

Mary   Dunno what you take me for . . . sort of person who'd sit here and be felt with people passing. If you won't stop I'll have to go down the back. (*She looks at him directly for the first time.*) If you won't stop.

Young Charlie (*not stopping; hoarsely*)   All right.

Mary (*looking off*)   Wait till that old fella goes past.

Young Charlie   Who?

Mary (*fondling his knee*)   Not that you're getting anything.

Young Charlie (*dazed with lust*)   I know.

Charlie   My silver-tongued eloquence had claimed its helpless victim. Defloration stared me in the face. My virginhood swung by a frayed thread. Then . . .!

Da (*off*)
'Oh, says your oul' one to my oul' one:
"Will you come to the Waxie Dargle?"
And says my oul' one to your oul' one:
"Sure I haven't got a farthin'."'

Young Charlie's *kneading and rubbing comes to a halt. As* **Da** *walks on at a good stiff pace, he tries to extract his hand from under* **Mary**'s *armpit but she holds it fast.*

(*Passing.*) More power. (*He walks a few more paces, stops, turns and stares.*) Jesus, Mary and Joseph.

Young Charlie (*his voice cracking*)   Hello.

Mary   Don't talk to him.

Da *looks at* **Mary**'s *hand on* **Young Charlie**'s *knee.* **Young Charlie** *removes her hand; she replaces it.*

Da Sure the whole world is going mad.

Mary Don't answer him.

Da *sits next to her.*

Da The whist drive was cancelled, bad scran to it. Only four tables. Says I: 'I'm at the loss of me tram fare down, but I won't be at the loss of it back, for I'll walk.' (*He looks at* **Young Charlie***'s hand flapping helplessly.*) I dunno. I dunno what to say.

Mary He'll go away. Don't mind him.

Charlie If my hand was free I'd have slashed my wrists.

Da Oh, the young ones that's going nowadays would eat you. I dunno.

Mary He doesn't know much.

Da He knows too shaggin' much. (*To* **Young Charlie**.) If your mother was here and seen the antrumartins of you, there'd be blood spilt.

Mary Much she'd care.

Da Much who'd care.

Mary Me ma.

Young Charlie He's talking to me.

Da Certainly I'm talking to him, who else? That's my young lad you're trick-acting with.

Mary (*to* **Young Charlie**) Is he your –

Da Oh, that's Charlie.

Mary Who?

Young Charlie Bruce is me middle name.

Da That's Charles Patrick.

Young Charlie Oh, thanks.

Da (*to* **Mary**)   You mind me, now. What is it they call you?

Mary (*a little cowed*)   Mary Tate.

Young Charlie   Leave her alone.

Da   You hold your interference. Mary Tate from where?

Mary   Glasthule . . . the Dwellin's.

Da *makes a violent gesture, gets up, walks away, turns and points at her dramatically.*

Da   Your mother was one of the Hannigans of Sallynoggin. Did you know that?

Mary   Yes.

Da   And your uncle Dinny and me was comrades the time of the Troubles. And you had a sister that died of consumption above in Loughlinstown.

Mary   My sister Peg.

Da   And another one in England.

Mary   Josie.

Da   Don't I know the whole seed and breed of yous! (*To* **Young Charlie**.) Sure this is a grand girl. (*He nudges* **Young Charlie** *off the bench and sits down next to* **Mary**.) Tell me, child, is there news of your father itself?

Mary (*her face clouding*)   No.

Da   That's hard lines.

Mary (*bitterly*)   We don't *want* news of him. Let him stay wherever he is – we can manage without him. He didn't give a curse about us then, and we don't give a curse about him now.

Da   There's some queer people walking the ways of the world.

Mary   Blast him.

Da *talks to her. She listens, nods, wipes her eyes.*

Charlie   And before my eyes you turned the Yellow Peril into Mary Tate of Glasthule, with a father who had sailed off to look for work in Scotland five years before, and had there decided that one could live more cheaply than seven. The last thing I'd wanted that evening was a person.

Da *rises, about to go.*

Da (*to* **Young Charlie**)   You mind your manners and treat her right, do you hear me. (*To* **Mary**.) Don't take any impudence from him. Home by eleven, Charlie.

Young Charlie   Yes, Da.

Da   'Bye-'bye, so. Mind yourself.

Mary   'Bye . . .

They watch until he is out of sight.

Your old fellow is great gas.

Young Charlie (*sourly*)   Oh, yeah. A whole bloody gasometer.

Mary (*pause*)   Well, will we go down the back?

Young Charlie   Uh . . . down the back . . . yeah.

Mary   He's gone, he won't see us. (*Affectionately, mocking.*) Bruce!

Young Charlie   The thing is, I promised Oliver I'd see him in the billiard hall.

Mary   Oh, yeah?

Young Charlie   Maybe some evening next week, if you're around, we can –

Mary   Mm . . . sure.

Young Charlie   Oliver's holding a table for us. Got to run. Well . . . see you.

Mary   Suppose you will. (*As he goes.*) Y'ought to wrap
yourself in cotton wool. (*Chanting.*) Daddy's little baby . . .
Daddy's little b—

She stops and begins to cry, then goes off.

Charlie   I stayed away from the sea-front for a long time
after that. (*He finds an object on the table in front of him.*) Is this
yours? (*He sees that he is alone. He looks at it more closely.*) Tug-o-
war medal. Nineteen . . . God almighty, nineteen-twelve. It
was different then. It was even different when . . . when?
When I was seven. You were an Einstein in those days.

Da *comes in from the scullery. He is thirty years younger: in his prime.*

Da (*a roar*)   Hup out of that! Put up your homework, get off
your backside, and we'll take the dog for a run around the
Vico.

Charlie (*happily*)   Yes, Da.

Da (*summoning the dog*)   Come on, Blackie . . . who's a good
dog? That's the fella . . . hup, hup! (*He crouches as if holding a
dog by the forepaws, and allows his face to be licked.*) Give us the
paw . . . give. Look at that . . . begod, wouldn't he near talk
to you? Get down. Are you right, son? (*He extends his hand.*)

Charlie *takes it.*

Mother *comes in from the scullery with a woollen scarf.*

Mother   No, he's not right. (*She puts the scarf around*
Charlie's *neck, tucking it in tightly.*) You have as much sense in
you as a don't-know-what. Dragging him out with his chest
exposed. Do you want to get him into bad health?

Charlie   Ah, Ma . . .

Mother   Ah, Ma! Go on. Bless yourselves going out, the
pair of you.

Charlie *and* **Da** *go into the hall.* **Da** *dips his fingers into a holy-
water font and flicks the water at* **Charlie**.

Da (*opening the front door: to the dog, stumbling*)   Blast you, don't trip me up . . . hoosh owa that!

They stop on the doorstep, **Da** *looking at the sky.*

During this scene, **Charlie** *does not attempt to imitate a child. He is an adult re-enacting a memory. Trust is evident in his attitude towards* **Da**.

That's a fine mackerel sky. Sure isn't it the best bloody country in the world!

Charlie   Da, say it.

Da   Say what?

Charlie   What you always say. Ah, you know . . . what the country mug in the army said. Say it.

Da (*feigning innocence*)   What did he say?

Charlie   Ah, do . . .

Da   Yis, well, he joins up. And sits down to his dinner the first night, and says he . . .

Charlie   Yeah, yeah!

Da   Says he: 'Yes, sir; no, sir; sir, if you please. Is it up the duck's arse that I shove the green peas?'

Charlie *laughs delightedly.*

They walk hand in hand up and around the stage, both singing 'Waxie Dargle'.

Lights go down on the kitchen. They stop at an upper level. **Da** *reaches back to help* **Charlie** *up.*

Come on, now . . . big step.

Charlie   I can't, Da.

Da   Yes, you can.

Charlie   I'll fall.

Da   You won't fall. Catch a hold of me hand. That's the lad . . . and there you go! Looka that, looka them mountains. There's a view, if you were rich enough you couldn't buy it. Do you know what I'm going to tell you? . . . there's them that says that view is better nor the Bay of Naples.

Charlie   Where's Naples, Da?

Da   Ah, it's in Italy.

Charlie   What's Italy like, Da?

Da (*pause, then gravely*)   Sticky, son . . . sticky.

Charlie   Da . . .

Da   What?

Charlie   Will I go to Italy when I grow up?

Da (*comforting*)   Not a fear of it . . . we wouldn't let you.

Charlie (*looking out and down*)   There's a ship. Is that it, Da? . . . is that our ship coming in?

Da   Where? No . . . no, son, that one's going out.

Charlie   Will ours come in tomorrow, Da?

Da   Begod now it might.

Charlie   We'll be on the pig's back then, Da, won't we? When we're rich.

Da   We won't be far off it.

Charlie   And what'll we do?

Da   Do?

Charlie   When we win the Sweep.

Da (*the standard answer*)   We won't do a shaggin' hand's turn.

Charlie (*awe and delight*)   Gawny!

Da (*deadpan*)   Sure the girl drew out me ticket the last time, and bad cess to her, didn't she drop it.

Charlie (*dismay*)   She didn't?

Da   She did.

Charlie   The bloomin' bitch.

Da   The what? Where did you hear that expression?

Charlie   I dunno, Da.

Da   Don't ever again let me hear you saying the like of that. That's a corner-boy expression.

Charlie   Sorry, Da.

Da   Women is different from you and me: y'ought to grow up to have respect for them. No, never call a woman a name like that, son, not even if she was a right oul' whoor. (*Pause.*) Do you know where we are now?

Charlie   Dalkey Hill, Da.

Da   Not at all. In my day this was called Higgins's Hill, and oul' Higgins used to chase us off it and him up on a white horse. He never set foot in church, chapel or meeting, and sign's on it when he died no one would have him, and (*Pointing off.*) that's where he's buried, under that stump of what's left of a cross after it was struck by lightnin'. Sure they say he sold his soul to the Oul' Fella himself.

Charlie   What oul' fella?

Da (*pointing down*)   Your man. Isn't the mark of his hoof on the wall below on Ardbrugh Road where he tripped running down to the mailboat to go back to England?

Charlie   Da, let's go home.

Da   What ails you?

Charlie   I'm afraid of old Higgins.

Da   Are you coddlin' me?

Charlie   And it's getting dark. I want to go home.

Da   Sure ghosts won't mind you if you don't mind them.

Charlie   Da . . . (*Reaching for his hand.*)

Da   Wait now till I light me pipe and then we'll go.

Charlie   Da, you know the thing I'm worst afraid of?

Da   What's that?

Charlie   Well, you know me mother? . . . not Ma: me real one.

Da   What about her?

Charlie   Me Aunt Bridgie says when it gets dark she comes and looks in at me through the window.

Da   Looks in at you?

Charlie   And she says she's tall and with a white face and a black coat, and she comes out from Dublin on the tram, and she wants me back.

Da   Is that a fact?

Charlie   And me Aunt Bridgie says it wasn't true what you told me when I was small, about me mother being on Lambay Island where she wasn't able to get hold of me, and living on pollack and Horny Cobblers.

Da   Not true? Did I ever tell you a word of a lie?

Charlie   I don't believe she's on Lambay Island.

Da   No. No, she's not there. That wasn't a lie, son: it was . . . a makey-up. Because you were too young, do you follow me . . . you wouldn't have understood.

Charlie (*apprehensive*)   Understood what? Why, where is she?

Da *looks impassively out to sea.*

Da, tell us.

Da (*seeming to change the subject*)   Do you see that flashing light?

Charlie   That's the Kish lightship.

Da   Well, that's where she is.

Charlie (*stunned*)   On the Kish?

Da   God help her.

Charlie   What's she doing on the Kish?

Da   She . . . cooks.

Charlie   For the lightshipmen?

Da   Yis.

Charlie   What does she cook?

Da   Ah, pollack, son, and Horny Cobblers.

Charlie *gives him a suspicious look, then peers out to sea.*

Charlie   Gawny.

Da   So now you know.

Charlie   Da . . . what if she got off the Kish? What if she's at home now before us and looking through the window?

Da   Well, if she is, I'll tell you what we'll do. I'll come up behind her and I'll give her the biggest root up the arse a woman ever got.

Charlie (*pleased*)   Will you, Da?

Da   I will. And bejasus it'll be nothing compared to the root I'll give your Aunt Bridgie. (*Rising, brushing his trousers-seat.*) Now where the hell is that whelp of a dog?

Charlie   Da, I love you.

Da (*staring at him in puzzlement*)   Certainly you do. Why wouldn't you? (*Moving away.*) Blackie, come here to me!

Da's *reply has the effect of causing* **Charlie** *to revert to his present-day self.*

Charlie (*fuming*)   Why wouldn't I? I'll tell you why bloody wouldn't I. Because you were an old thick, a zombie, a mastodon. My God . . . my mother living on a lightship, trimming the wick and filleting Horn Cobblers. What a blazing, ever-fertile imagination you had – Cobblers aren't even edible!

Da (*whistles*)   Blackie!

Charlie   And pollacks!

Da   You're right son, that's what he is.

Charlie   The black dog was the only intelligent member of the family. He died a few years later. He was poisoned, and no one will convince me it wasn't suicide. God knows how Ma ever came to marry you.

Lights came up in the kitchen. **Mother** *looks on while* **Young Charlie** *is writing a letter.*

Oh, I know how, sort of . . . she told me. I mean why.

Mother   He was called Ernie Moore. He used to be on the boats . . . the B and I. The 'Lady Hudson-Kinahan' it was. I was very great with him for a while. Then himself came to the house one day and said how he had the job above in Jacob's and he wanted to marry me. So that was that.

Young Charlie   How?

Mother   It was fixed.

Young Charlie   How fixed?

Mother   My father told him I would, so it was fixed. Things was arranged in them days.

Young Charlie   Did you want to?

Mother   I had no say in it.

Young Charlie   How well did you know him?

Mother   Well enough to bid the time of day to.

Young Charlie   That was handy.

Mother   A body's not put into this world to pick and choose and be particular. I was seventeen, I done what I was told to.

Young Charlie   What about Popeye the Sailor?

Mother   Who?

Young Charlie   The other one.

Mother   Mr Moore in your mouth. When your time comes and you have to answer to God in the next world it makes no differ who you married and who you didn't marry. That's when everything will be made up to us.

Young Charlie   You mean they hand out free sailors?

Mother   What? You little jeer, you. (*She aims a blow at him which he wards off.*) Well, God send that you never have to get married young for fear that if you stayed at home you might die, like many another died, of consumption for want of proper nourishment.

Young Charlie *affects to ignore her. He resumes writing and sings 'Popeye the Sailorman' under his breath in derisive counterpoint.*

Waited on hand and foot, never wanting for nothing. Well, when you do get married, to whatever rip will have you, I only hope you'll be half the provider for her as himself has been for me. Is that letter done?

Young Charlie   Yeah.

Mother   Read it out.

Young Charlie   The Jacobs don't care whether I got a job or not.

Mother   It's manners to tell them, they ask after you. Go on.

Young Charlie   'Dear Nelson and Jeanette . . .'

She gives him a look. He amends.

'Dear Mr and Mrs Jacob: My father has told me how often
you have been so good as to inquire as to whether I have yet
found employment. I am grateful for your interest and am
glad to say that I have now been given a clerical position.
So, happily, I am no longer like Mr Micawber, constantly
expecting something to turn up. Thanking you for your–'

Mother   What sort of codology is that?

Young Charlie   What?

Mother   You're no longer like who?

Young Charlie   It's an expression out of a book.

Mother   Write it out again and do it proper.

Young Charlie   What for?

Mother   Because you're told to.

Young Charlie   Look, there's this character in a book.
He's always hard up, but he's an optimist. He –

Mother   Do as you're bid.

Young Charlie   There's nothing wrong with it. Maybe
you don't understand it, but the Jacobs will. It's meant to be
funny, they'll laugh when they read it.

Mother   Aye, to be sure they will. At you, for setting
yourself up to be something you're not.

Young Charlie   It's my letter. You're not writing it: I am.

Mother   Then write it proper.

Young Charlie   Proper-*ly*.

Mother   Don't you pull *me* up. Don't act the high-up lord
with *me*, not in this house. They said I'd rue the day, and the
gawm I was, I didn't believe them. He'll turn on you, they
said. My own mother, me good neighbours, they all –

Young Charlie   Oh, play another record.

Mother   Don't you back-answer me, you cur.

Young Charlie   Whatever it is, if you don't understand it, it's rubbish. To hell with Charles Dickens and the rest of them. Nat Gould and Ruby M. Ayres made the world.

Mother   Are you going to write that out again, yes or no?

Young Charlie   No, because there's nothing the –

Mother   Are you not! (*She looks up at* **Da**, *who with* **Charlie** *is still standing in the hill area.*) Nick . . .

Da   Ah, son, write it out the way she wants you to.

Mother   Don't beg him: tell him.

Da (*violently*)   Will you do as you're bloody well told and not be putting the woman into a passion! Can we not have a solitary minute's peace in the house with you and your curse-o'-God Jack-acting?

Mother   Do that letter again.

Young Charlie (*in a rage*)   All right, all right! I'll do it. (*He crumples up the letter, takes the notepad and writes furiously.*) 'Dear Mr and Mrs Jacob . . . I am very well. My parents hope you are well, too, as it leaves them. I have a j-o-b now. I do not know myself, I am that delighted. Thanking you and oblige . . .' (*He signs it.*) Now are you happy?

Mother   Hand it here. I wouldn't trust you to post it. (*She takes the letter and puts it into an envelope. He cannot quite believe that she is taking it seriously.*)

Young Charlie   You're not going to send –

Da (*turning to* **Charlie**)   Begod, son, you always made a great fist of writing a letter.

Young Charlie (*barely in control*)   I'm going to the billiard hall.

Mother   Go wherever you like.

Young Charlie *storms out, loudly singing 'Popeye the Sailorman'. He emits a last mocking 'Boop-boop!' as he vanishes. We hear the far-off barking of a dog.*

Charlie   It was a long time before I realized that love turned upside down is love for all that.

Da   There's the whoorin' dog gone down ahead of us in the finish. And the lights is on in the town. (*Pointing.*) That's the Ulverton Road, son, where we frightened the shite out of the Black-and-Tans. And the lamp is lit in your uncle Paddy's window.

Charlie   If it is, he didn't light it: he's dead these donkey's years. Uncle Paddy, Kruger Doyle, Gunjer Hammond, Oats Nolan – all your cronies – and old Bonk-a-bonk with his banjo and Mammy Reilly in her madhouse of a shop, with her money, so they said, all in sovereigns, wrapped up inside her wig. All dead. Like yourself . . . and, trust you, last as usual.

Da   That's a hash old wind starting up. We'll need a couple of extra coats on the bed tonight, son.

Charlie   We will.

Da   Mind your step now. If you slip and cut yourself she'll ate the pair of us. Give me your hand. Let the light from the Kish show you where the steps are.

Charlie   That's it, Mother: light us home. Least you can do.

Curtain.

Act Two

Charlie *and* **Young Charlie** *appear, walking towards the front door. There is a slightly exaggerated vivacity in* **Charlie**'s *manner: the result of having had a few drinks.*

Charlie Ikey Meh? I remember the *name* . . .

Young Charlie The tram conductor. We used to yell Ikey Meh at him when the tram went past, and he'd pull the emergency stop and lep off after us –

Charlie Leap off.

Young Charlie . . . And leave the passengers high and dry. God, he could run.

Charlie Of course: yes! Ikey Meh. *('Meh' is drawn out in imitation of a goat.)* He – *(He catches sight of* **Da**, *who is trailing along behind them.)* I told you to stop following me. Now go away.

Young Charlie Leave him alone.

Charlie I go out for a bite to eat and a quiet jar, to get away from him, and what happens? He's in the pub ahead of me. Fizz off.

Da *hangs back and lurks in the shadows.*

Young Charlie You might be civil to him. I mean, it's his day.

Charlie It was. The funeral's over.

Young Charlie *(coldly)* Oh, that's exquisite. You're a gem, you are.

Charlie Don't get uppish with me, sonny Jim: you're as dead as he is. Come in and keep me company while I finish up.

Young Charlie I think I'll hump off.

Charlie (*aggressively*)   You'll hump nowhere. You'll stay in my head until I choose to chase you out of it.

Young Charlie   Oh, will I?

Charlie   There's only room in there for one of you at a time, and if I let you leave he'll come back like a yo-yo. Look at him, lurking. Get in there when you're told to. (*He has opened the front door with a key and pushes* **Young Charlie** *in ahead of him.*)

Young Charlie   Mind who you're shaggin' pushin'.

Charlie   Shag*ging*. Push*ing*. Get in.

Da *comes up to the door, moving fast.*

Oh, no you don't. Out, and stay out. (*He shuts the door.*)

Da *promptly walks through the fourth wall and sits in his armchair filling his pipe.*

Young Charlie   Someone to see you.

Charlie   Who? (*He stares angrily at* **Da**.)

Da   God, they done wonders with the public house, son. I wouldn't recognize it. All the metally bits and the red lights . . . it'd put you in mind of a whoorhouse.

Young Charlie   When were you ever in a –

Charlie   Say nothing. Ignore him. (*He searches through the bureau drawers.*)

Da   That pub used to be called Larkin's . . . you didn't know that.

He fetches a jug from the dresser and empties it. It is filled with old keys, bits of yarn and thread, receipts, newspaper clippings, odds and ends.

Young Charlie   If you hadn't gone out you could have been finished and away by now. But no, you couldn't wait to get maggoty drunk.

Charlie   Maggoty? On three small ones?

Da   I never seen you take a drink before, son. But sure what odds? Aren't you old enough?

Young Charlie (*primly*)   *I* never needed artificial stimulets.

Charlie   Stimulants.

Young Charlie   Booze. Look at you.

Da (*placidly*)   The way you swally-ed them. Begod, says I to meself, that fellow would drink Lough Erin dry.

Charlie   Shut up. (*To* **Young Charlie**.) What's wrong with me?

Young Charlie   Well, you're a bit of a disappointment.

Charlie   Oh, yes?

Young Charlie   I mean, I'd hoped to do better for meself.

Charlie   What had you in mind?

Young Charlie   Don't get huffy. It's not that I amn't glad to see you: at least it means I'll live till I'm forty: that's something.

Charlie   Thanks.

Young Charlie (*looking at* **Charlie**'*s wrist*)   And I like the watch.

Charlie   Oh, good.

Young Charlie   I suppose I could have done worse: but you can't deny you're a bit ordinary. It gives a fellow the creeps, seeing himself at your age: everything behind him and nothing to look forward to.

Charlie   I get the old-age pension next year: there's that.

Young Charlie   Yesterday I was thinking: I'm only eighteen, anything can happen to me . . . anything. I mean, maybe a smashing girl will go mad for me. Now I dunno.

Charlie *puts on his glasses to read a receipt.* **Young Charlie** *looks at him.*

Ah, God.

Charlie   What?

Young Charlie   Glasses. I'm blind as well.

Charlie   I'm sorry about that. The time I was castrated in a car crash, it affected my eyesight.

Young Charlie (*horrified*)   You weren't. (*Then.*) You're so damn smart.

Da   Oh, them motor cars is dangerous.

Young Charlie   Everything's a laugh, isn't it? Anyone I see who's your age . . . same thing. All lah-de-dah and make a joke of it. God if something good happens to me, I jump up in the air, I let out a yell, I run. Your sort just sits there.

Charlie   Arthritis.

Young Charlie   You're dried up. Dead.

Charlie   I'm a seething torrent inside.

Young Charlie   You? You're jizzless.

Charlie   I'm what?

Young Charlie   There's no jizz in you. The fun's gone out of you. What's worse, you're no good . . . wouldn't even take him with you to London when me ma died.

Charlie   I asked him.

Young Charlie   Instead of forcing him.

Charlie   Him? Who could force him to do anything?

Young Charlie   Did you try?

Charlie   Don't get righteous with me, my pasty-faced little friend. It doesn't become you. Were *you* any good?

Who was it once gave him a packet of six razor blades for Christmas?

Young Charlie   I was broke.

Charlie   Yeah, and why? Because you'd bought a pair of nylons for that typist from Cappoquin who let you grope her up against the railings of the Custom House. Six Gillette blades!

Da   Oh, there was great shaving in them blades.

Young Charlie   You weren't even here when he died.

Charlie   It was sudden.

Da (*rising*)   I think I have one of them still. Hold on.

Charlie, Young Charlie (*together*)   Sit down.

Charlie   It was sudden. I'm not clairvoyant.

Young Charlie   You were glad it was sudden, though, weren't you?

Charlie   Why not? It's the best way. No pain . . .

Young Charlie   No pain for you, you mean. No having to go to him and wait and watch him and say things. All the dirty bits over with when you got here.

Charlie   Do you think I planned it?

Young Charlie   No, but it suited you. Didn't it?

Charlie   I was . . .

Young Charlie   Relieved.

Charlie (*nodding*)   Mm.

Young Charlie   Look at me, you with your lousy watch. I haven't got a tosser, but at least I've got a few principles. Where's yours?

Charlie   Principles? You mean like when you took that job Drumm offered you?

Young Charlie   That's a stop-gap.

Charlie   I see.

Young Charlie   I'll be out of it in a month and doing what I want to.

Charlie   A month?

Young Charlie   A month!

Drumm *appears in the neutral area, a letter in his hand.*

Drumm   My friend . . . (*As* **Young Charlie** *looks around.*) Come in here.

Young Charlie   Now what? (*He leaves the kitchen through the fourth wall and goes over to* **Drumm**.) Yes, Mr Drumm?

Drumm   How long have you been employed here?

Young Charlie   Thirteen years, Mr Drumm.

Drumm   In those thirteen years it may not have escaped your notice that there is one filing drawer for names with the initial letter 'M', and another for those which are adorned with the prefix 'Mac', whether written M-a-c, M-c or M-apostrophe. This letter pertains to one James Maguire. I found it, after a forty-minute search, in the 'Mac' drawer. Spell 'Maguire', would you?

Charlie, Young Charlie (*together*)   M-a-g-u-i-r-e.

Drumm (*slowly, as if it were a death sentence*)   M-a-g.

Young Charlie   I must have –

Drumm   M-a-g.

Young Charlie   Yes.

Drumm   You will concede that this was incorrectly filed?

Young Charlie   Technically, yes . . .

Drumm (*with venom*)   Don't use words you don't know the meaning of. A barely literate child could have filed this letter where it belongs. But not, apparently, a man thirty years of age, with a wife, the beginnings of a family and pretensions towards intellectual superiority.

Young Charlie   That has nothing to do with – (*He stops.*)

Drumm (*dangerously*)   With whom? (*He nods towards the other, unseen members of the staff.*) Get on with your work. (*To* **Young Charlie**.) With whom?

Young Charlie (*a retreat*)   With this place.

Drumm *smiles at him scornfully.*

Drumm   File this where it –

Young Charlie   Or with you either, Mr Drumm.

Drumm   Don't get insolent with me, my friend. If you don't like it here, be off with you. No one is holding you. But while you remain you will stay awake and do your work. Accurately. Do you understand?

Young Charlie *holds out his hand for the letter.*

I asked if you understood.

Young Charlie   Yes. (*He takes the letter.*)

Drumm   We all know that you think your position here is beneath you. But you must try and put up with it and with us, Mr Tynan. Or whatever your name is.

Young Charlie *looks at him, then goes.* **Drumm** *remains standing during the following.*

Da   Oh, Old Drumm is a decent man.

Charlie   For years he'd taken me in hand like a Victorian father. He taught me, not by his enthusiasms – he had none – but by his dislikes.

Drumm   Women, Mr Tynan, should be given a damn good squeeze at the earliest opportunity, and thereafter avoided.

Charlie   Perhaps he wanted a son or had a fondness for strays. He made me his confidant.

Drumm   That man Kelly is known to be a pervert. Shun him. What's more, he spits as he talks. I move away from him, and he follows me and spits on me again.

Charlie   One evening, I was in a hurry somewhere – to meet a girl, go to a film: I don't know. I saw him coming towards me. I didn't want to stop and talk, so I crossed over. He'd seen me avoid him. It was that simple. Except at work, he never spoke to me again.

*The light fades on **Drumm**. **Da** gets the razor blade from the bureau.*

Da   Ah.

Charlie   What?

Da   I dunno is this one of the blades you gev me, son.

Charlie   Show. (*He sniffs at it.*) A Gillette, definitely. Sheffield, I'd say . . . nineteen-forty-three. An impudent blade, sharpish aftertaste . . . precocious, but not presumptuous. Damn it, I bet this *is* one of them. Anything I ever gave you, you took and wouldn't use. Wouldn't be under a compliment to me.

Da *slips the blade into **Charlie**'s pocket.*

Da   Say nothing . . . take them home with you.

Charlie   It's a wonder you cashed the cheques I sent you for tobacco.

Da   Certainly I cashed them. Wasn't that how I got thrun out of that home you put me into last January?

Charlie   Home? Blast your impudence, that was a private hotel.

Da   Whatever it was.

Charlie   I'm telling you what it was. An hotel.

Da (*carelessly*)   Yis.

Charlie   Because you'd gone dotty. Shouting out to Ma, who was two years dead. Going around to my cousin Rosie for your Christmas dinner at two in the morning. Do you know how hard it was to get you into that hotel?

Da   Hotel my arse. Sure they wouldn't let me go up to the bank to cash that cheque you sent me. But begod, says I, I'll bate them yet. Do you know what I done?

Charlie   I heard.

Da   I got out over the shaggin' wall. And these two big impudent straps of country ones cem after me. 'Come back,' says they. 'Leave go of me,' says I; 'The divil's cure to the pair of yiz.' Then doesn't one of them put her mawsy red hands on me be the collar. 'Be a good boy,' says she to me. Well . . . (*He laughs fondly.*) I drew out with me fist and I gev her a poke for herself in the stomach.

Charlie   They told me it was on the breast.

Da   I wouldn't poke a woman in the breast.

Charlie   You did *something*.

Da   I gev her a root.

Charlie   A what?

Da   Where were you brung up? A kick, a kick. And after that you had me put into the Union.

Charlie   Into the what?

Da (*ashamed to say it*)   You know . . . the . . . the . . . the poorhouse.

Charlie   Oh, you malignant, lop-sided old liar. It was a private room in a psychiatric hospital.

Da   I know, I know.

Charlie   A hospital.

Da Yis.

Charlie (*incredulous*)   Poorhouse!

Da Sure it's greatly improved since I was a young lad. You wouldn't know a bit of it.

Charlie (*beginning to shout*)   It was not the p—

Da I amn't saying a word again' it. Sure hadn't I the best of everything, and wasn't I better off there than I was where you put me before that – in that home?

Charlie (*giving up*)   Jesus.

Da Do you know what I'm going to tell you? If the oul' heart hadn't gone on me the evenin' before last, I'd be alive today.

Charlie Is that so?

Da It is.

Charlie There are no shallows to which you won't sink, are there?

Da (*proudly*)   There aren't! (*Reminiscent.*) You never seen me when I was riz, did you, son?

Charlie No. (*Then.*) Yes . . . once.

Da You did not.

Charlie Nineteen-fifty-one. You were sixty-seven . . . She was sixty-three then, and I still don't believe I saw it happen.

There is a squeak of the gate and **Mother** *appears. She is carrying a shopping bag.*

Da (*looking out*)   There she is at long last. It's gone half-past six; I thought she was run over. (*He opens the door.*)

Mother *comes in. She is in a good mood, humming to herself.*

I say, we thought you were under the wheels of a bus. Where were you at all? The boy is home before you, with his stomach roaring for his tea.

Mother (*unruffled*)   He'll get it when it's put in front of him, not before. (*She takes off her coat and hangs it up, then puts on her apron.*)

Da (*grumbling*)   We didn't know *what* happened to you. Was the picture any good itself?

Mother   It was an old love thing, all divorces and codology. A body couldn't make head or tail of it. Charlie, clear that rubbidge off the table and be a bit of help to me.

Charlie *puts the odds and ends back in the jug.*

Mother *begins to lay the table.*

Da   It's seldom we hear a song out of you.

Mother   I ought to cry to suit you.

Da   I'm only saying, any other time the picture is a washout you come home to us raging. (*Pause.*) And your horse finished down the field today as well.

Mother   Did it? (*Nodding, not caring.*) The going was too soft.

She goes on with her work, still humming.

Charlie and **Da** *exchange puzzled looks.*

Da (*curious, fishing*)   I suppose Dun Laoghaire was packed.

Mother   Crowds.

Da   Nothing strange or startling, so?

Mother (*almost coyly*)   Mm . . .

Da   Well, tell us or don't tell us, one or the other.

Mother *turns. She cannot keep her adventure to herself.*

Mother   I was treated to a glass of port in the Royal Marine Hotel.

Da   You were what?

Mother   Someone I met in Lipton's.

Charlie   The grandeur of you!

Da (*laughing*)   Was he good-looking itself?

Mother   It wasn't a 'him' at all – don't be such a jeer.
This woman comes up to me. 'Excuse me,' says she, 'for
asking. Are you not Margaret Tynan . . . Maggie Doyle,
that was?' 'I am,' says I; 'Do I know you?' 'You do,' says
she.

Da (*in disgust*)   Ah.

Mother   Well, to cut a long story, who was she but Gretta
Moore out of the Tivoli in Glasthule.

Da   I never heard tell of her.

Mother   Ah, Gretta Nolan that married Ernie Moore off
of the B and I.

Charlie (*remembering*)   Who?

Mother   He's retired these two years.

Charlie (*it comes to him; singing*)   'I'm . . . Popeye the
Sailorman!'

Mother   Hold your tongue.

Da *is staring at her, numbed.*

So in with the pair of us into the Royal Marine Hotel. Says
she to me: 'Sure we're as good as the best of them.' And the
style of all the old ones there, with their dyed hair and the
fur coats on them. Tea, they were all having, and sweet
cake. 'Sure,' says Gretta, 'we can have *that* at home in the
house.' (*To* **Charlie**.) So this waiter comes up in a swalla-
tail coat. Oh, she was well able for him. 'We want two large
glasses of port wine,' says she, and off he went like a hare to
get them!

Da   Making a show of yourself.

Charlie   What show?

Da   High-up people looking at you!

Mother (*loftily*)   Pity about them!

Da   The whole town'll have it tomorrow

Charlie (*to* **Mother**)   Then what?

Mother   Three shillings for two glasses of port wine you'd be hard put to it to wet your lips with . . . and sixpence on top of that for the waiter. Oh, it was scandalous. Says I to her –

Da   Sure Ernie Moore is dead these donkey's years.

Mother   What?

Da (*dogged*)   I know he's dead.

Mother   How do you know?

Da   I know.

Mother   The man's wife says different.

Da   Oh aye, ask me brother am I a liar! Oh, she must be a right good thing. And you're worse. Pouring drink into you in the Royal Marine Hotel, and the crowds of the world looking at you and . . . and . . . laughing.

Charlie   What crowds?

Mother   Don't mind him.

Da   And I say he's dead and long dead.

Mother   Is he? Well, I'll soon tell you next Thursday whether he's dead or no.

Da   What's next Thursday?

Mother (*almost coquettishly*)   I'm invited down for me tea.

Da   Down where, for your tea?

Mother   To the Tivoli. (*To* **Charlie**.) Gretta was telling me her eldest is beyant in Canada, and she has a grandson nearly your age, and –

Da   Well, you'll go there by yourself if you go, because I'm staying where I am.

Mother   You can stay wherever you like, for you weren't invited.

Da   Am I not!

Mother   Your own tea will be left here ready for you.

Da   Well, it needn't be, because you're not going.

Mother   Why amn't I?

Da   You aren't setting foot outside of here.

Mother   You won't stop me.

Da   Will I not!

Mother (*her fury mounting*)   You were always the same and you always will be the same. The one time I'm invited to a person's house, you begrudge it to me. (*Beginning to shout.*) Well, I'll go *wherever* I like and see *whoever* I like.

Da   Do, and you'll go out of this. I'm the boss in this house and I'll stay the boss in it.

Charlie   She's only going for a cup of tea.

Da (*wildly*)   Oh aye . . . aye, that's what she'd like us to think. But it's to see him . . . *him*.

Mother   To see who?

Da   You faggot, you: don't let on you don't know. It's Ernie . . . Ernie . . . curse-o'-God Ernie! (*His fist crashes on the table.*) May he die roaring for a priest . . . curse-o'-God Ernie!

Even **Mother**, *who knows him, is alarmed by the violence of his rage. She stares at him. He strikes the table again.*

Charlie (*remembering*)   And the floorboards barked like dogs, and the cups went mad on their hooks.

Da   You set one foot in the Tivoli, you look crossways at a whoor-master the like of him, and be Jesus, I'll get jail for you, do you hear me? I won't leave a stick or a stone standing in the kip.

Mother (*recovering, still a little afraid*)   Look at you . . . look at the yellow old face of you.

Da (*savagely, almost skipping with rage*)   With your . . . your port wine, and your sweet cake, and your Royal Marine Hotel.

Mother   The whole town knows you for a madman . . . aye, and all belonging to you.

Da   Ernie . . . Ernie! You'll stay clear of him, Thursday and every other day.

Mother   Because you know I preferred him over you, and that's what you can't stand. Because I never went with you. Because you know if it wasn't for me father, God forgive him, telling me to –

Da *makes a violent rush at her, his fist raised.*

Charlie   Hey . . .

Da'*s fist comes down and stops, almost touching her face, where it stays, trembling, threatening.*

Mother (*quietly*)   Go on. Go on, do it. And that'll be the first time and the last. I'll leave here if I was to sleep on the footpath.

Pause. **Da** *starts past her towards the scullery.*

(*Half to herself.*) You went behind my back to him because you knew I wouldn't have you.

Da *runs to the table and raises a cup as if to dash it to pieces. Instead, he takes his pipe from the table and throws it on the ground. It breaks. He goes into the scullery.* **Charlie** *stoops to pick up the pieces of the pipe as* **Mother** *faces away from him to wipe her eyes.*

Charlie (*still stooping*)   Will you go? On Thursday?

She faces him. Although tears are coming, there is a wry, almost mocking attempt at a smile.

Mother   The jealous old bags.

The lights fade. Then we see a woman enter and sit on a rustic seat in the neutral area. She is **Mrs Prynne***, 50, Anglo-Irish accent, dressed for the country.*

Young Charlie (*off, singing: the tune is 'Blaze Away'*)
'Tight as a drum,
Never been done,
Queen of all the fairies!'

Mrs Prynne *opens her eyes. Through the following,* **Young Charlie** *comes on carrying two quart cans.*

'Bolicky Biddy had only one diddy
To feed the baby on.
Poor little fucker had only one sucker
To grind his teeth up . . .' (*He stops on seeing* **Mrs Prynne**.)

Mrs Prynne   Good evening. Do you know where Tynan is? The gardener.

Young Charlie   He's in the greenhouse. Will I tell him you want him?

Mrs Prynne   If you would.

Young Charlie   Sure. (*He goes across the stage.*) Da! Hey . . .

Da *appears, carrying a basket of tomatoes.*

You're wanted.

Da   Who wants me?

Young Charlie   I dunno. Posh-looking old one.

Da (*a mild panic*)   It's the mistress. Hold this for me . . . will you hold it! (*He thrusts the basket at* **Young Charlie** *and getting his coat from offstage struggles to put it on.*)

Young Charlie   Easy . . . she's not on fire, you know. (*Helping him.*) How much do you think?

Da　How much what?

Young Charlie　Money.

Da (*confidently*)　I'll get me due. Poor oul' Jacob wouldn't see me stuck, Lord ha' mercy on him . . . no, nor none of us. Says he many's the time: 'Yous'll all be provided for.' The parlourmaid and Cook got their envelopes this morning. (*A sob in his throat.*) A decent poor man.

Young Charlie　Don't start the waterworks, will you?

Da (*voice breaking*)　God be good to him.

Young Charlie　Hey, is it true they bury Quakers standing up?

Da　Jasus, you don't think they do it sitting down, do you? Where's the mistress?

Young Charlie　Yours or mine? (*As* **Da** *looks at him.*) By the tennis court. (*He calls after him.*) Da . . . how much was the cook left?

Da　A hundred.

Young Charlie　Pounds? (*He emits a quiet 'Yeoww!' of pleasure.*)

Exits. **Da** *makes his way painfully, carrying the basket of tomatoes. He salutes* **Mrs Prynne**.

Mrs Prynne　Oh, Tynan, isn't this garden beautiful? Mr Prynne and I shall hate not to see it again. I'm sure you'll miss it too. Sit down, Tynan: next to me.

Da *salutes and sits beside her.*

We loathe selling 'Enderley', but with my dear father gone and the family with homes of their own, there's no one left to live in it.

Da　I picked you the best of the tomatoes, ma'am.

Mrs Prynne   Aren't you the great man. We'll take them back to Mountmellick with us in the morning. And the rose-trees.

Da (*authoritative, tapping her knee*)   Yis . . . now don't forget: a good pruning as soon as you plant them. Cut the hybrids – the Peer Gynts, the Blue Moons and the Brasilias – cut them well back two buds from the bottom, and the floribundas to five buds.

Mrs Prynne   The floribunda to five buds.

Da   The harder you cut, the better the bloom: only don't cut into a stem that's more than a year old.

Mrs Prynne (*attentive*)   I'll remember.

Da (*slapping her knee*)   I'll make a rose-grower out of you yet, so I will. And feed the buggers well in July, do you hear, if you want a good second bush.

Mrs Prynne   I do hope they take: my father loved the Enderley roses. Did you hear we have a buyer for the house, Tynan? A schoolteacher and his wife. She owns a fashion business in the city . . . I daresay that's where their money is. Catholics, I believe.

Da (*contemptuous*)   Huh!

Mrs Prynne   I'm sure they'll want a gardener.

Da   Let them. Catholics with money, letting on they're the Quality: sure they're the worst there is. No, I wouldn't work for me own: they'd skin you. The way it is, the legs is gone stiff on me, and the missus says it's time I gev meself a rest.

Mrs Prynne   What age are you now, Tynan?

Da   I'm sixty-eight, and I'm here since I was fourteen.

Mrs Prynne   Fifty-four years?

Da   The day yourself was born, the master called me in. Nineteen-hundred-and-three, it was. 'Take this in your hand, Tynan,' says he to me, 'and drink it.' Begod, I never seen a tumbler of whiskey the size of it. 'And now,' says he, 'go off to hell home for the rest of the day.'

Mrs Prynne   The world is changing, Tynan, and not for the better. People are growing hard; my father's generation is out of fashion.

Da's *eyes are moist again. She takes an envelope from her handbag.* **Da** *gets to his feet.*

In his will he asked that Mr Prynne and I should attend to the staff. We think you should have a pension, Tynan: you're entitled to it. We thought twenty-six pounds per annum, payable quarterly.

Da (*saluting automatically*)   Thanks, ma'am; thanks very much.

Mrs Prynne   Nonsense, you've earned it. Now, the lump sum. Poor Cook is getting on and will have to find a home of her own, so we've treated her as a special case. But I'm sure you and Mrs Tynan won't say no to twenty-five pounds, with our best wishes and compliments.

Da *takes the envelope and again salutes automatically. He looks at it dumbly.*

You're a great man for the work, and whatever you may say, we know you wouldn't give it up for diamonds. And there's that boy of yours. Once he leaves school he'll be a great help to you. You did well to adopt him.

Da   The way it is, do you see, the young lad is saving up to get married . . .

Mrs Prynne   Married?

Da   So we'd think bad of asking him to –

Mrs Prynne   How old is he?

Da   Sure didn't yourself send him up to get me.

Mrs Prynne   Was that he? But he's a young man.

Da (*calling*)   Charlie! Come here to me. (*To* **Mrs Prynne**.)
Sure he's working these six years. Only every shilling he
earns, do you see, has to be put by. So herself and me, we
couldn't ask him to –

Mrs Prynne   You mustn't encourage him to be selfish.
Young people can live on next to nothing. (*As* **Young
Charlie** *arrives*.) Hello. How d'you do?

Young Charlie   'Evening.

Da   Shake hands now, son. (*To* **Mrs Prynne**.) He cem to
pick the loganberries. Sure we couldn't leave them to go
rotten.

Mrs Prynne   You are thoughtful. I'll ask Cook to make
jam and send it to us in Mountmellick. (*To* **Young
Charlie**.) I hear you're getting married.

Young Charlie   I hope to.

Mrs Prynne   Well done. But you must look after this old
man. Remember how much you owe him, so be good to
him, and generous. (*She looks in her handbag and finds a five-
pound note*.) Mr Prynne and I would like you to have this. A
wedding gift. Perhaps you'll buy something for your new
home.

Young Charlie   No . . . thank you. I –

Da   Yes, he will. Take it.

Young Charlie   Well . . . (*Taking it*.) I'm sure we could do
with a Sacred Heart picture for over the bed.

Da (*missing the sarcasm*)   That's the boy!

Mrs Prynne   I see you've reared an art-lover, Tynan.
And now the most important thing. I know my father would
want you to have a keepsake . . . one of his treasures. (*She
picks up a loosely-wrapped package from the seat*.

Da *and* **Charlie** *are intrigued*.

(*To* **Young Charlie**.) Have you travelled?

Young Charlie   Not much.

Mrs Prynne   You must. In these days of aeroplanes, young people have no excuse. When my father was your age he'd been around the world. In nineteen-hundred-and-six he was in San Francisco at the time of the earthquake. That's on the west coast of America, you know.

Young Charlie   Yes, I saw the film.

Mrs Prynne   After the great fire, he was passing a gutted jewellery shop when he saw this, lying on the ground for the taking. A find in a thousand, Tynan. (*She reverently lifts the paper, unveiling a mass of tangled bits of wire mounted on a metal base.*) What do you think of that? Thirty or more pairs of spectacles, fused together by the heat of the fire. (*Pause.*) My father had them mounted.

Da   Sure, what else would he do with them?

Mrs Prynne   Extraordinary, yes?

Da   That's worth having.

Mrs Prynne   It is, and there you are. (*She gives it to him; then shaking hands.*) Goodbye, Tynan. Take care of yourself and we'll call to see you when we're in town. (*To* **Young Charlie**.) See that he doesn't overdo things, won't you? Goodbye . . . our best to your intended. (*She goes off, taking the various cans with her.*)

Da *salutes her, tears in his eyes.*

Young Charlie   It's a miracle she didn't take the bench. When she said he found it in the ruins of a jeweller's shop, I thought for sure it was the Star of India. Thirty pairs of spectacles.

Da   You hold them: me hands is dirty. Don't drop them.

Young Charlie   Don't what?

Da   They're worth money.

Young Charlie (*irate*)   Ah, for – What are you bawling for?

Da   A great man, she said I was. Sure I am, too.

Young Charlie   How much did you get?

Da   Fifty-four years in the one place. I laid that tennis court . . . aye, and rolled it, too.

Young Charlie   I don't care if you knitted the net. How much?

Da (*looking up*)   And I planted them trees.

Young Charlie (*realizing*)   You've been diddled.

Da   What diddled? Sure she needn't have gev me anything. The work I done, wasn't I paid for it . . . every Friday like a clockwork. I got me week off in the summer . . .

Young Charlie   Give me that. (*He takes the envelope and opens it.*)

Da (*unheeding, ranting away*)   And me two days at Christmas, with an extra pound note put into me fist, and the sup of whiskey poured and waiting for me in the pantry. Wasn't I –

Young Charlie (*looking at the cheque*)   Twenty-five?

Da (*snatching it back*)   Don't go tricking with that.

Young Charlie   Is that *it*?

Da   Isn't it money for doing bugger-all? And sure haven't I the offer of work from the people that's bought the house.

Young Charlie   What work? You're giving it up.

Da   Ah, time enough to give it up when I'm going downhill. Catholics, yis. They own a dress shop. Sure if your own won't look after you, who will?

Young Charlie   My God, she'll kill you.

Da   Who will?

Young Charlie   She will, when you bring that home to her. (*Meaning the cheque.*) Here, put this with it. (*He offers him the five-pound note.*)

Da   What for?

Young Charlie   It'll save you a couple of curses.

Da   Go 'long out of that . . . that's for yourself and Polly, to buy the holy picture with. Are you off into town to see her?

Young Charlie   Well, I'm not going home, that's for sure. Blast her anyway, and her twenty-five quid and her Californian wire puzzle.

Da   Sure the Quakers was the only ones that was good to us the time of the Famine. Oh, the mistress is a decent skin. (*He laughs.*) 'Tynan,' says she to me, 'aren't you the greatest man that ever trod shoe-leather!' And I planted them hyacinths, too.

Young Charlie *has gone off, taking the parcel with him.*

Da *goes into the house.*

Mag . . . Mag. Do you know what the mistress said to me?

Lights up. **Charlie**, *his glasses on, is writing. The jug, with its contents, is back on the table.*

Charlie   Twenty-five pounds divided by fifty-four. I make it that your gratuity worked out at nine shillings and threepence per year of service. No wonder she didn't talk to you for a week.

Da   Who didn't?

Charlie   She didn't.

Da   Are you mad? In fifty-nine years there was never a cross word between us.

Charlie   Oh, dear God.

Da   There was not.

Charlie   'Ernie, Ernie, curse-o'-God Ernie!'

Da   Sure I was only letting on I was vexed with her. (*With relish.*) Oh, I put a stop to her gallop, her and her . . . high tea! Son, do you remember them spectacles from San Francisco?

Charlie   Do I?

Da   Herself took them down to the pawn office. 'How much will you give me on these?' says she. 'I'll give you nothing at all on them, ma'am,' says he, 'for they're too valuable for me to keep under this roof.' And you saying I was diddled: you thick, you!

Charlie   Where are they?

Da   What?

Charlie   The spectacles.

Da (*shiftily*)   I musta lost them.

Charlie   Liar. (*Searching.*) They're in this house, and if I find them, I'll pulp them and bury them. You ignorant, wet, forelock-tugging old crawler. (*Mimicking him.*) 'Begod, ma'am, sure after fifty-four years all I needed to be set up for life was a parcel of barbed wire.' And then you put in another four years, toiling for the Catholic but somewhat less than Christian Diors of Grafton Street.

Da   'Tynan,' says that bitch's ghost to me, and him only a school-master, 'I want more honest endeavour from you and less excuses.' 'Do you see this fist?' says I to him –

Charlie (*still searching*)   I asked you where they were.

Da   I disrecall.

Charlie   You probably had them buried with you. I can hear St Peter now – 'Hey God, there's an old gobshite at the tradesmen's entrance with thirty pairs of spectacle-frames from the San Francisco earthquake. What'll I tell him?' (*God's voice, with a Jewish accent.*) 'Tell him we don't want any.'

(*He scoops up the contents of the jug and moves to dump them in the range.*) Mind up: this is the last.

Da (*seizing on an article*)   That pipe is worth keeping.

Charlie   It's in bits. You broke it.

Da   Sure a piece of insulating tape would –

Charlie   No. Move. (*He goes past* **Da** *and drops the lot in the range.*)

Da   You could have smoked that, and you'll folly a crow for it yet. What else did you throw out? (*He opens* **Charlie**'s *dispatch case and goes through the papers.*)

Charlie   At the funeral this morning I heard one of your old cronies muttering what a great character you were and how I'll never be the man me da was.

Da   Don't belittle yourself: yes, you will. What's this?

Charlie   Death certificate. Tell me, what was it like?

Da   What?

Charlie   Dying.

Da (*offhand*)   Ah, I didn't care for it. (*Peering at a document.*) Eighteen-hundred-and-

Charlie   Eighty-Four. Birth certificate.

Da (*annoyed*)   You kept nothing worth keeping at all. There was more to me than this rubbidge. Where's me old IRA service certificate? And the photograph of the tug-o'-war team? I still have the mark under me oxter where the rope sawed into it. And the photo herself and meself had took in the Vale of Avoca.

Charlie   I threw them out.

Da   And yourself the day of your first Communion with me beside you.

Charlie   I burned them. I don't want them around.

Da *stares blankly at him.* **Charlie** *waits, almost daring him to be angry.*

Da   You wha'?

Charlie   I got rid of them. You're gone, now they're gone. So?

Da (*nodding*)   Ah, sure what the hell good were they anyway.

Charlie   Eh?

Da   Bits of paper. Sure they only gather dust.

Charlie   I burned all that was left of you and you can't even get angry. You were a sheep when you lived: you're still a sheep. 'Yes, sir; no, sir; sir, if you please –'

Da (*chuckling*)   'Is it up the duck's arse that I shove the green peas?' Oh, that was a good poem. (*Singing.*) 'Is it up the –'

Charlie   Where's my coat? I'm going to the airport.

Da   Yis. (*Calling.*) Mag . . . Mag, the lad is off.

Charlie   She won't answer you. Goodbye.

Mother *comes in quickly from the scullery. She pays* **Charlie** *no attention.*

Mother (*briskly*)   Where is he? (*Calling upstairs.*) Charlie, you'll be late. (*To* **Da**.) Call him.

Da (*yelling*)   You pup, will you come down before the shaggin' aeroplane is off up into the air and you're left standin'!

Mother   Charlie!

Da   If he misses that aeroplane they'll be no whoorin' weddin'. Then he'll be nicely destroyed. Jasus, come when you're called!

Young Charlie, *carrying a suitcase, is on the stairs, followed by* **Oliver**.

Mother   That will do. He won't miss it.

Young Charlie (*coming in*)   Will you quit roaring. I'm not deaf.

Mother   It's the last time you'll have to put up with it, so hold your tongue. Have you everything?

Young Charlie   Yes.

Mother   Smarten yourself. Anyone'd think it was Oliver that was getting married.

Oliver   Oh, now. Ho-ho. Oh, now.

Young Charlie   I left Oliver's wedding present upstairs. Will you keep it for me?

Oliver   It's just a bowl to float rose-petals in-you-know. Maybe your da will give you some of his roses.

Da   I only grow the shaggers. I don't learn 'em to swim.

Mother   You're to mind yourself in that aeroplane and bless yourself when it starts.

Young Charlie   Yes.

Da   Oh, Charlie won't crash.

Mother (*half snapping*)   No one is saying to the contrary.

Da   Divil a fear of him.

Mother (*aggrieved*)   Going off to the other side of the world to get married.

Young Charlie   Five hundred miles . . .!

Mother   It's far enough. Too far.

Young Charlie   It's where she lives.

Da   Oh, Belgium is a great country.

Mother   It's little you or I will ever see of it. No matter.

Young Charlie (*angrily*)   Don't start. You were both invited –

Mother   Oh, aye. Aye, I'm sure we were.

Young Charlie (*to* **Oliver**)   They damn well were. But no, it's too far, it's too foreign, his legs won't let him . . .

Mother   I said it's no matter.

Young Charlie *gives her a hostile look.*

Oliver   When he gets time during the honeymoon, Charlie is going to drop you a line and give me all the details.

As they look at him.

About going in an aeroplane-you-know.

Pause. **Young Charlie** *is chafing to be off and trying to conceal it.* **Charlie** *moves to be near him.*

Mother   You may as well be off, so. There's nothing to keep you.

Young Charlie (*protesting*)   I'll be back in a fortnight.

She nods, upset.

Mother   Please God.

Charlie   Now. Goodbye, and out.

Young Charlie   Yeah, well, mind yourselves.

Mother   You mind yourself. (*She reaches for him blindly.*)

He half-resists the kiss, half-accepts it. She steps back and looks at him, eyes large. He reaches for his case as **Da** *comes forward, hand extended.*

Charlie   Hang on . . . one to go.

Da (*shaking hands*)   Good luck now, son. Sure you'll get there in grcat style. Oh, aeroplanes is all the go these days.

Young Charlie   Yeah. 'Bye, now.

Da (*not letting go*)   Have you your tickets?

Young Charlie   Yes.

Charlie (*to* **Da**)   Let go.

Da   Have you your passport?

Young Charlie   Yes.

Charlie   It's the Beast with Five Fingers.

Da   Have you your –

Young Charlie   I've got to go. (*He prises his hand free and starts out.*)

Mother   Bless yourself!

He dips his fingers in the holy-water font and hurries out. **Mother** *and* **Da** *come to the door.* **Oliver** *is caught behind them. He coughs.*

Oliver   I'm going with him. As far as the bus-you-know.

Young Charlie (*agonized, waiting for him*)   For God's sake.

Oliver   Well, 'bye-'bye now and sappy days. That's an expression him and me have-you-know. Oh, yes.

Young Charlie (*half to himself*)   Oliver!

Oliver (*turning to wave*)   Cheerio, now.

Charlie (*from the house*)   Well, at least wave to them.

Young Charlie *raises a hand without turning and climbs across to an upper level where he rests, waiting for* **Oliver**.

Oliver   That went well, I thought. I mean, they can get very sentimental-you-know. Often with my mother I can't feel anything because I'm trying to stop *her* from feeling anything. How do *you* feel?

Young Charlie *makes a huge gesture of relief.*

They're all the same-you-know. I dread the roars of my mother when I get married. She cries even if I go to a late-night dance.

Young Charlie   Come on before we meet someone.

Oliver   Oh-ho. Off to the altar. Can't wait.

Young Charlie   Dry up.

Oliver   The eager bridegroom. Oh, yes.

Young Charlie   Well, it's the beginning, isn't it?

They go off.

Mother   Well, that's the end of him. (*She and* **Da** *return to the kitchen.*)

Da   Still and all, mebbe we ought to have gone, Mag, when we were asked.

She gives him a sour look.

Sure it'd have been a . . . a . . . a change for us.

Mother   I never hindered him. I wasn't going to start now.

Da   What hinderment? Weren't we asked?

Mother (*it is not a disparagement, but evasion*)   You'd be a nice article to bring to a foreign country. (*Then.*) I think I'll make his bed now and have done with it. (*She goes upstairs. She is in view during part of the following.*)

Da (*laughing, watching her*)   Oh, a comical woman.

Charlie   She died an Irishwoman's death, drinking tea.

Da   Do you want a cup?

Charlie   No! Two years afterwards, I told a doctor in London about you, on your own and getting senile. I said you'd have to be made to come and live with us. He said: 'Oh, yes. Then he can die among strangers in a hospital in Putney or Wandsworth, with nothing Irish around him except the nurses. But with your luck you'd probably have got Jamaicans.' It's always pleasant to be told what you half-want to hear. So when I came to see you – the last time – there was no talk of your going to London. I was solicitous: asked you how you were managing, were you eating regularly . . .

Da *is in his 80s, stooped and deaf.* **Charlie***'s attitude is paternal.*

Da   Hoh?

Charlie   I said are you eating regularly?

Da   Sure I'm getting fat. I go to Rosie for me tea and Mrs Dunne next door cooks me dinner. Are *you* eating regular?

Charlie   She's a widow. I'd watch her.

Da   Hoh?

Charlie   I say I'd watch her.

Da   I do.

Charlie   You reprobate. Do you need extra cash, for whist drives?

Da   I gave up going. Me hands is too stiff to sort the cards into suits. The last time I went, oul' Drumm was there. Do you remember oul' Drumm?

Charlie   Yes.

Da   He accused me of renegin'. 'Why don't you,' says he, 'join the Old People's club and play there?' Says I to him back: 'I would,' says I, 'only I'm too shaggin' old for them!' (*He laughs.*)

Charlie   That was good.

Da   Sure I have the garden to do . . . fine heads of cabbage that a dog from Dublin never pissed on. I'm kept going. I say I blacked the range yesterday.

Charlie   You're a marvel.

Da   I am. How's all the care?

Charlie   They're great. Send their love.

Da (*rising*)   I was meaning to ask you . . .

Charlie   What?

Da (*saluting him*)   I do often see your young one in the town.

Charlie   What young one?

Da   Her . . . Maggie. Your eldest. 'Clare to God, Mr Doyle, I never seen such shiny bright hair on a girl.

Charlie *stares at him.*

Note: this is not a flashback to **Da** *as a young man; it is* **Da** *in his 80s, his mind wandering.*

Sure she's like a young one out of the story books. The way it is, Mr Doyle, I'm above at Jacob's these six years, since I was fourteen. I have a pound a week and the promise of one of the new dwellin's in the square. I'd think well of marrying her, so I would.

Charlie   Da, no, she's –

Da   You can ask anyone in the town about me. And, and, and she wouldn't want for an'thing. The job is safe, we won't go short. I'm learning roses, do you see. To grow them. Oh, yis: Polyanthas and Belles de Crecys and Cornelias and Tuscanys and Amy Robsarts and Janet's Prides and –

Charlie   Da, stop.

Da   And, and, and Portlands and Captain John Ingrams and Heidelbergs and Munsters and Shepherdesses and Golden Jewels and Buccaneers and New Dawns and King's Ransoms and –

Charlie   Jesus Christ, will you stop. (*In despair.*) You old get, what am I going to do with you?

Da   A rainbow of roses. I never seen a young one like her . . . so I know you'd think bad of refusing me. (*Looking at* **Charlie**.) But sure you wouldn't.

Charlie   No.

Da   And you'll put in a good word for me? She wouldn't go again' you.

Charlie   I'll talk to her.

Da (*happy now*)   I'm on the pig's back, so. On it for life. Oh, she won't be sorry. (*Looking up at the ceiling.*) Mag! Mag, are you up there?

Charlie   Da, sh. (*He seats* **Da**.)

Da (*begins to sing aimlessly*)
'I've just been down to Monto Town
To see the bould McArdle,
But he wouldn't give me half a crown.
To go to the Waxy –'

Charlie   Stop it: it's not then any more, it's now. (*Picking up a paper.*) See that? Death certificate . . . yours.

Da *nods and straightens up, returning to the present.* **Charlie** *puts the papers back into his dispatch case and closes it.*

Da   I never carried on the like of that.

Charlie   How?

Da   Astray in the head. Thinking it was old God's time and you were herself's da.

Charlie   Oh, didn't you!

Da   And not a bit like him. Begod, I don't wonder at you putting me into the poorhouse.

Charlie (*getting annoyed again*)   You useless old man.

The gate squeaks.

Da   Sure it must have gev you a laugh, anyway.

Charlie *is too angry to speak. He picks up his overcoat.*

Da *moves to assist him.*

Drumm *appears outside the house carrying a briefcase. He is now 70, still erect.*

Are you off, so? Well, God send you good weather, son. Tell them I was asking for them.

Drumm *knocks at the front door.*

That must be another Mass card. Do you know, I have enough of them to play whist with.

As **Charlie** *goes to the door.*

Did you see the flowers on me coffin? . . . Shaggin' weeds, the half of them. (*He sits.*)

Charlie *opens the door.*

Charlie (*surprised*) Mr Drumm . . .

Drumm I'm glad I caught you. Might I have a word?

Charlie Of course . . . come in.

They go into the kitchen.

Da Oh, old Drumm is not the worst of them.

Drumm It's been many years. Will you agree to shake hands? . . . it's a bad day for grievances.

They do so.

There, that's done . . . I'm obliged. Mind, I won't say it's generous of you: *I* was the wounded party.

Charlie It was a long time ago.

Drumm (*good-humoured*) Don't play word-games with me, my friend. Time doesn't mitigate an injury; it only helps one to overlook it. (*Indicating a chair.*) May I?

Charlie Please.

Drumm (*sitting*) Years ago I made a choice. I could have indiscriminate friendships or I could have standards. I chose standards. It's my own misfortune that so few people have come up to them.

Charlie Including me.

Drumm You tried. You had your work cut out.

Charlie I had.

Drumm (*being fair*) I daresay I was difficult.

Charlie Impossible.

Drumm (*bridling*) And you've become impudent.

Charlie (*unruffled*) Yes.

Drumm A beggar on horseback.

Charlie It's better than walking.

Da There was a young fella went to confession. 'Father,' says he, 'I rode a girl from Cork.' 'Yerra, boy,' says the priest, 'sure 'twas better than walking.'

Charlie's *face twitches.* **Drumm** *glares at him.*

Charlie I hope you're well.

Drumm Your hopes are unfounded.

Charlie Oh?

Da Didn't I tell you he was sick? Sure he has a face on him like a boiled –

Charlie (*hastily*) It's hard to believe. You look well.

Drumm *chuckles to himself as if at a private joke. He leans confidentially towards* **Charlie**.

Drumm I have this . . . tummy trouble. I told a certain person – I don't know why, out of mischief, it isn't like me – I told him cancer was suspected. Quite untrue. Of course he told others, and since then my popularity has soared. I said to one man: 'I know you for a rogue and a blackguard.' Was he offended? 'You're right,' he said; 'come and have a drink.' (*With defiant pleasure.*) I did.

Charlie   There'll be ructions when you don't die.

Drumm   There will.

Charlie   False pretences.

Drumm   Pity about them.

Charlie   Still . . .

Drumm   They shun a man because he's intelligent, but get maudlin over a few supposedly malignant body-cells. I'm as bad. Ten years ago I wouldn't have given one of them the time of day, still less have taken pleasure in their approbation.

Charlie   Do you?

Drumm   People like them, like the old man – your foster-father – they thank God for a fine day and stay diplomatically silent when it rains. They deride whatever is beyond them with a laugh, a platitude and a spit. They say: 'How could he be a dental surgeon? – his father was warned by the police for molesting women.'

Da   Who would that be? Old Martin Conheedy used to tamper with women. Is his son a dentist now?

Drumm (*answering* **Charlie**'*s question*)   They . . . amuse me.

Da (*derisive*)   Who'd trust that fella to pull a tooth?

Drumm (*picking up his briefcase*)   When the old man was in hospital he sent word that he wanted to see me.

Charlie   My father?

Drumm   Who lived here.

Charlie (*persisting*)   My father.

Drumm (*letting it pass*)   He asked my advice. I told him that not being related by blood you would have no natural claim on his estate.

Charlie   What estate? He had nothing.

Drumm   At his request I wrote out a will for him then and there. He signed it and I had it witnessed. (*He takes an envelope and hands it to* **Charlie**.) It'll stand up with the best of them.

Charlie   But he had bugger-all.

Drumm   There was also the matter of an heirloom which he gave into my keeping.

Charlie   Heirloom?

Drumm *dips into his briefcase and takes out a familiar-looking brown-paper parcel.*

Da (*jovially*)   There now's a surprise for you.

Charlie (*staring at the parcel*)   No . . .

Da (*crowing*)   You won't guess what's in that!

Drumm   He said it was valuable, so I asked my bank manager to keep it in his vault.

Charlie (*under stress*)   *That* was in a bank vault?

Drumm   I can see that the value was also sentimental. (*Rising.*) Well, I'm glad to have discharged my trust.

Charlie   Thank you. (*Looking at the parcel.*) His estate.

Drumm   Oh, no. Whatever that is, it has nothing to do with what's in the will. And I'd be careful with that envelope. There's money involved!

Charlie   Money?

Drumm   He mentioned the sum of a hundred and thirty-five pounds, with more to come.

Charlie   He never had that much in his life.

Drumm   He thought otherwise.

Charlie   He was raving. I *know*. All he had was his pension and the cheques I sent him for – (*He breaks off and looks around at* **Da**.)

Da (*strategically*)   That dog from next door is in the garden. Hoosh . . . hoosh, you bastard.

Charlie *watches him murderously as he beats a retreat into the scullery.*

Drumm (*waiting for* **Charlie** *to finish*)   Yes?

Charlie   I was wrong. I've remembered where it came from.

Drumm   The money?

Charlie   Yes.

Drumm   I imagined it was hard-earned.

Charlie (*grimly*)   It was.

Drumm (*sternly*)   Now, my friend, no caterwauling. To whom else could he leave it? I once called him an ignorant man. I still do. And yet he may have been better off. Everything I once thought I knew for certain I have seen inverted, revised, disproved, or discredited. Shall I tell you something? In seventy years the one surviving fragment of my knowledge, the only indisputable poor particle of certainty in my entire life, is that in a public house lavatory incoming traffic has the right of way. (*Acidly.*) It isn't much to take with one, is it?

Charlie (*smiling*)   Well, now *I* know something.

Drumm   I have always avoided him and his kind, and yet in the end we fetch up against the self-same door. I find that aggravating. (*Moving towards the door.*) The old couple, had they children of their own?

Charlie   I was told once there were several. All still-born.

Drumm   He didn't even create life – at least I have the edge on him there.

Charlie   How are the two Rhode Island Reds?

Drumm   Moulting. (*He offers his hand.*) It was pleasant to see you. I enjoyed it. Goodbye.

Charlie   Mr Drumm, he never took anything from me, he wouldn't let me help him, what I offered him he kept and wouldn't use. Why?

Drumm   Don't you know?

Charlie   Do *you*?

Drumm   The Irish national disease.

Charlie   Bad manners?

Drumm   Worse, no manners. (*He holds out his hand, inspecting the sky for rain, then goes.*)

Charlie *closes the door, returns to the kitchen.*

Charlie   Where are you? (*Yelling.*) Come . . . in . . . here!

Da *comes in.*

Da   Do you want a cup of tea?

Charlie   You old shite. You wouldn't even use the money.

Da   I did.

Charlie   How?

Da   Wasn't it something to leave you?

Charlie   I'll never forgive you for this.

Da (*not worried*)   Ah, you will.

Charlie   Since I was born. 'Here's sixpence for the chairoplanes, a shilling for the pictures, a new suit for the job. Here's a life.' When did I ever get a chance to pay it back, to get out from under, to be quit of you? You wouldn't come to us in London; you'd rather be the brave old warrior, soldiering on.

Da   And wasn't I?

Charlie   While I was the ingrate. The only currency you'd take, you knew I wouldn't pay. Well, I've news for you, mate. You had your chance. The debt is cancelled, welshed on. (*Tapping his head.*) I'm turfing you out. Of here. See that? (*He tears the black armband from his overcoat and drops it in the range.*) And this? (*He holds up the parcel containing the spectacle frames.*)

Da   You wouldn't. Not at all.

Charlie   Wouldn't I? You think not? (*He bends and crushes the frames through the paper with increasing violence.*)

Da   Ah, son . . .

Charlie   San Francisco earthquake!

Da   You'd want to mind your hand with them –

Charlie (*cutting his finger*)   Shit.

Da   I told you you'd cut yourself.

Charlie *gives him a malevolent look and very deliberately shoves the parcel into the range. He sucks his hand.*

Charlie   Now wouldn't I?

Da   Is it deep? That's the kind of cut 'ud give you lockjaw. I'd mind that.

Charlie   Gone . . . and you with it.

Da   Yis. (*Taking out a dirty handkerchief.*) Here, tie this around it.

Charlie   Get away from me. Ignorant man, ignorant life!

Da   What are you talking about, or do you know what you're talking about? Sure I enjoyed meself. And in the wind-up I didn't die with the arse out of me trousers like the rest of them – I left money!

Charlie   *My* money.

Da   Jasus, didn't you get it back? And looka . . . if I wouldn't go to England with you before, sure I'll make it up to you. I will now.

Charlie   You what? Like hell you will.

Da   Sure you can't get rid of a bad thing.

Charlie   Can't I? You watch me. You watch!

He picks up his case, walks out of the house and closes the front door. He locks the door and hurls the key from him. A sigh of relief. He turns to go, to find **Da** *has walked out through the fourth wall.*

Da   Are we off, so? It's starting to rain. The angels must be peein' again.

Charlie   Don't you dare follow me. You're dead . . . get off.

Da   Sure Noah's flood was only a shower. (*Following him.*) Left . . . left . . . I had a good job and I left, right, left!

Charlie   Hump off. Get away. Shoo. I don't want you.

He goes to the upper level. **Da** *follows, lagging behind.*

Da   Go on, go on. I'll keep up with you.

Charlie *stops at the top level.*

Charlie   Leave me alone.

Charlie *slowly walks down as* **Da** *follows, singing.*

Da (*singing*)
'Oh, says your oul' one to my oul' one:
"Will you come to the Waxy Dargle?"
And says my oul' one to your oul' one:
"Sure I haven't got a farthin'."'

Curtain.